COMMENTARIES ON
"THE LIFE DIVINE"

The Mother

COMMENTARIES ON "THE LIFE DIVINE"

(Two of the Last Chapters)

SRI AUROBINDO ASHRAM
PONDICHERRY

First edition 1994
Second edition 2017

Rs 145
ISBN 978-93-5210-134-4

© Sri Aurobindo Ashram Trust 1994, 2017
Published by Sri Aurobindo Ashram Publication Department
Pondicherry 605 002
Web http://www.sabda.in

Printed at Sri Aurobindo Ashram Press, Pondicherry
PRINTED IN INDIA

Publisher's Note

This book comprises the Mother's oral commentaries on two of the last chapters of *The Life Divine*, Sri Aurobindo's principal work of spiritual philosophy. The commentaries were given in 1957 and 1958 to members of the Mother's Wednesday Class, held weekly at the Playground of the Sri Aurobindo Ashram. The class consisted of a large gathering of Ashram members and students of the Ashram's school. After reading out a portion of the text, the Mother would answer any questions raised in the class. Though she did not systemetically discuss all the subjects in the chapters, she did cover most of their central ideas.

The commentaries deal with the two chapters titled "Man and the Evolution" and "The Evolution of the Spiritual Man", and the beginning of a third chapter, "The Triple Transformation". The Mother intended to comment on all the last six chapters, but a serious illness intervened, resulting in the ending of the class.

The commentaries have been reproduced from pages 209-431 of *Questions and Answers 1957-1958*, Volume 9 of the second edition of the Collected Works of the Mother.

Contents

On "Man and the Evolution"

1957

23 October	Central motive of existence. Evolution	3
30 October	Double movement of evolution. Disappearance of a species	9
13 November	Superiority of man over animal. Consciousness precedes form	16
27 November	Sri Aurobindo's method of exposition. Individual and cosmic evolution	27
4 December	Sri Aurobindo's, method of exposition. Emergence of a new species	31
11 December	Appearance of the first man	38
18 December	Modern Science. Experience gives power. The supramental power	42

1958

1 January	The collaboration of material Nature. Miracles	47
Appendix	Explanation of 1958 New Year Message	50

8 January	Sri Aurobindo's method of exposition. Mental organisation and control	53
15 January	The only unshakable point of support	61
22 January	Action and speculation. Expressing the real truth	63
29 January	The plan of the universe. Self-awareness	66
5 February	The great voyage of the Supreme. Freedom and determinism	72
12 February	Psychic progress from life to life	77
19 February	The supramental boat experience	80
Appendix	The "Censors". Absurdity of artificial means	90
26 February	The moon and the stars. Horoscopes and yoga	96
5 March	Vibration and words. Power of thought. The gift of tongues	99
12 March	The key of past transformations	106
19 March	Tension, Peace and Progress. Human perversion	110
26 March	Mental anxiety and worry	117
2 April	Correcting a mistake	124
9 April	The eyes of the soul	126
16 April	The superman. The new realisation	129

23 April	Progress and bargaining	136
30 April	Mental constructions and experience	137

On "The Evolution of the Spiritual Man"

7 May	The secret of Nature	144
14 May	Intellectual activity limited. Supramental life	150
21 May	Mental honesty	153
28 May	The Avatar	158
4 June	New birth	163
11 June	Spiritual being in everyone	168
18 June	Religion, occultism, philosophy. Spiritual experience	171
25 June	Sadhana in the body	178
9 July	Faith and personal effort	182
16 July	Is religion a necessity?	186
23 July	Developing intuition. Concentration	190
30 July	Automatic writing. Occultism	196
6 August	Collective prayer. Ideal collectivity	203
13 August	Profiting by staying in the Ashram. What Sri Aurobindo has come to tell us	208
15 August	Our relation with the Gods	214

27 August	Meditation and imagination. From thought to idea to principle	216
3 September	How to discipline the imagination	223
10 September	Magic, occultism, physical science	231
17 September	Power of formulating experience. Usefulness of mental development	242
24 September	Living the truth. Words and experience	250
1 October	The ideal of moral perfection	256
8 October	Stages between man and superman	259
22 October	A reversal of consciousness. Helping others	262
29 October	Mental limitations. Grace	268
5 November	Knowing how to be silent	273

On "The Triple Transformation"

12 November	The aim of the Supreme. Trust in the Grace	278
26 November	The role of the Spirit. New birth	283

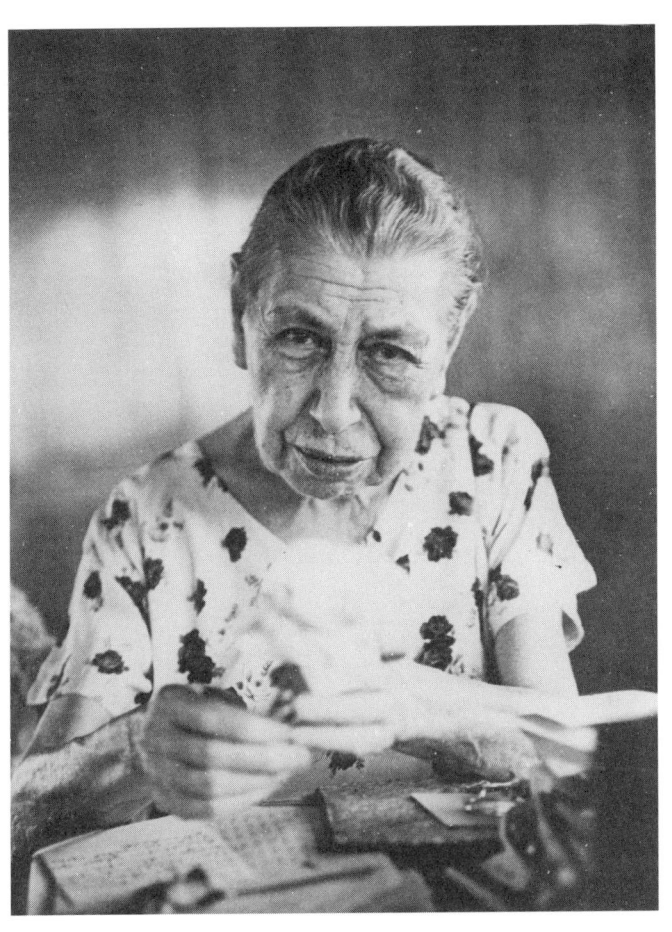

THE MOTHER

COMMENTARIES ON "THE LIFE DIVINE"

(Two of the Last Chapters)

23 October 1957

Mother begins the reading of the last six
chapters of *The Life Divine*.

> *"A spiritual evolution, an evolution of consciousness in Matter in a constant developing self-formation till the form can reveal the indwelling Spirit, is then the key-note, the central significant motive of the terrestrial existence. This significance is concealed at the outset by the involution of the Spirit, the Divine Reality, in a dense material Inconscience; a veil of Inconscience, a veil of insensibility of Matter hides the universal Consciousness-Force which works within it, so that the Energy, which is the first form the Force of creation assumes in the physical universe, appears to be itself inconscient and yet does the works of a vast occult Intelligence."*
> The Life Divine, SABCL, Vol. 19, p. 824

I didn't understand, Sweet Mother, what this Consciousness-Force was, so I did not understand anything!

The first thing to understand is precisely this first sentence which states the fact, the raison *d'être* and the very principle of universal existence. You see, we are beginning here at the end of the volume, these are the last six chapters. Throughout the beginning of the book

Sri Aurobindo has taken one after another all the theories explaining the how and why of the universe and of existence; he has carried them to their extreme limits in order to explain fully what they mean, and at the end he has shown how far they were incomplete or imperfect and given the true solution. All that is, as it were, finished with; it lies behind our reading. It would have taken us something like ten years to go through all that! And you would have required all kinds of knowledge and a great intellectual development to be able to follow it with any profit. But for our part, we are beginning from where he has shown, from the purely intellectual point of view, what the purpose of existence is, and he formulates it like this: "the central significant motive of the terrestrial existence." For he is not concerned with the entire universe, he has taken terrestrial life, that is, our life here on Earth, as a symbolic and concentrated representation of the purpose of the entire universe. In fact, according to very old traditions, the Earth, from the deeper spiritual point of view, has been created as a symbolic concentration of universal life so that the work of transformation may be done more easily, in a limited, concentrated "space" — so to say — where all the elements of the problem are gathered together so that, in the concentration, the action may be more total and effective. So here he speaks only of terrestrial existence, but we can understand that it is a symbolic existence, that is, that it represents a universal action. It is a symbolic, concentrated representation. And he says that "the central motive", that is, the purpose of terrestrial existence is to awaken, to develop and finally to reveal in a total manifestation the Spirit which is hidden at the centre of Matter and impels this Matter from within outwards towards a progressive development which will liberate the Spirit working from within.

So, in the outer appearances as you see them, at first you find the mineral kingdom with stones, earth, minerals which to us, in our outer consciousness, appear absolutely unconscious. Yet, behind this unconsciousness there is the life of the Spirit, the consciousness of the Spirit, which is completely hidden, which is as if asleep — though that is only an appearance — and which works from within in order gradually to transform this Matter that is completely inert in appearance, so that its organisation may lend itself more and more to the manifestation of consciousness. And he says here that at first this veil of inert Matter is so total that, to a superficial glance, it is something that has neither life nor consciousness. When you pick up a stone and look at it with your ordinary eyes and consciousness, you say, "It has no life, no consciousness." For one who knows how to see behind appearances, there is, hidden at the centre of this Matter — at the centre of *each atom* of this Matter — there is, hidden, the Supreme Divine Reality working from within, gradually, through the millennia, to change this inert Matter into something that is expressive enough to be able to reveal the Spirit within. Then you have the progression of the history of Life: how, from the stone there suddenly appeared a rudimentary life and through successive species a sort of organisation, that is, an organic substance capable of revealing life. But between the mineral and vegetable kingdoms there are transitional elements; one doesn't know whether they belong to the mineral or already to the vegetable kingdom — when one studies this in detail one sees some strange species which belong neither here nor there, which are not quite this and yet not quite that. Then comes the development of the vegetable kingdom where naturally life appears, for there is growth, transformation — a plant sprouts up, develops, grows — and with the first phenomenon of life comes also the phenomenon of decomposition and disintegration which is relatively much more rapid than in the stone: a stone, if protected from the impact of other forces, can last apparently indefinitely, whereas the plant already follows a curve of growth, ascent and decline and decomposition — but this with an extremely restricted consciousness. Those who have studied the vegetable kingdom in detail are well aware that there is a consciousness there. For instance, plants need sunlight to live — the sun represents the active energy which makes them grow — so, if you put a plant in a place where there is no sunlight, you see it always growing up and up and up, trying, making an *effort* to reach the sunlight. In a virgin forest, for instance, where man does not interfere, there is this kind of struggle among all the plants which are always growing straight upwards in one way or another in their *effort* to catch the sunlight. It is very interesting. But even if you put a flower-pot in a fairly small courtyard surrounded by walls, where the sun doesn't come, a plant which normally is as high as this (*gesture*), becomes as tall as that: it stretches up and makes an *effort* to find the light. Therefore there is a consciousness, a will to live which is already manifesting. And little by little, with species that are more and more developed, you again reach another transitional passage between what is no longer entirely a plant and still not yet an animal. There are several species like that, which are very interesting. There are those plants which are carnivorous, plants like an open mouth: you throw a fly inside, snap! they swallow it. It is no longer quite a plant, it is not yet an animal. There are many plants of this kind.

Then you come to the animal. The first animals, yes, it is difficult to distinguish them from plants, there is almost no consciousness. But there you see all the animal species, you know them, don't you, right up to the higher animals which, indeed, are very conscious. They have their own completely independent will. They are very conscious and marvellously intelligent, like the elephant, for instance; you know all the stories about elephants and their wonderful intelligence. Therefore, it is already a very perceptible appearance of mind. And through this progressive development, we suddenly pass on to a species which has probably disappeared — traces of which have been found — an intermediate animal like a monkey or of the same line as the monkey — something close to it, similar, if not the monkey as we know it — but already an animal that walks on two legs. And from there we come to man. There is an entire beginning of the evolution of man; we can't say, can we, that he shows a brilliant intelligence, but there is already an action of the mind, a beginning of independence, of independent reaction to the environment and the forces of Nature. And so, in man there is the whole range, right up to the higher being capable of spiritual life.

That is what Sri Aurobindo tells us on this page. That is all. Now, if you have a question to ask?...

> *Sweet Mother, here he says: "This consciousness... reaches its climax of intelligence and exceeds itself in Man...."*

Yes, that is what I have just told you: at his highest stage, man begins to be altogether independent of Nature — "altogether" is an exaggeration: he can become altogether independent. A man who has realised the spiritual consciousness in himself, who has a direct relation with the divine Origin is literally independent of Nature, of the force of Nature.

(*It begins to rain.*) Ah! That is to cool down our minds! (Laughter)

And that is what he calls "exceeding itself", that is, that the Being, the inner divine Consciousness, the supreme spiritual Reality in its effort to develop... (*It rains harder.*) Oh, oh! We shall have to stop talking... in its effort to develop a conscious means of manifesting itself has arrived at a being capable of having a direct contact with It without going through the whole process of Nature.

Now, I think we are going to stop. No meditation, because...

30 October 1957

"This terrestrial evolutionary working of Nature from Matter to Mind and beyond it has a double process: there is an outward visible process of physical evolution with birth as its machinery, — for each evolved form of body housing its own evolved power of consciousness is maintained and kept in continuity by heredity; there is, at the same time, an invisible process of soul evolution with rebirth into ascending grades of form and consciousness as its machinery. The first by itself would mean only a cosmic evolution; for the individual would be a quickly perishing instrument, and the race, a more abiding collective formulation, would be the real step in the progressive manifestation of the cosmic Inhabitant, the universal Spirit: rebirth is an indispensable condition for any long duration and evolution of the individual being in the earth-existence. Each grade of cosmic manifestation, each type of form that can house the indwelling Spirit, is turned by rebirth into a means for the individual soul, the psychic entity, to manifest more and more of its concealed consciousness; each life becomes a step in a victory over Matter by a greater progression of consciousness in it which shall make eventually Matter itself a means for the full manifestation of the Spirit."

The Life Divine, SABCL, Vol. 19, pp. 825-26

It is difficult to understand, Sweet Mother.

Ah!...

If you take terrestrial history, all the forms of life have appeared one after another in a general plan, a general programme, with the addition, always, of a new perfection and a greater consciousness. Take just animal forms — for that is easier to understand, they are the last before man — each animal that appeared had an additional perfection in its general nature — I don't mean in all the details — a greater perfection than the preceding ones, and the crowning point of the ascending march was the human form which, for the moment, from the point of view of consciousness, is the form most capable of manifesting consciousness; that is, the human form at its height, at the height of its possibilities, is capable of more consciousness than all preceding animal forms.

This is *one* of Nature's ways of evolution.

Sri Aurobindo told us last week that this Nature was following an ascending progression in order to manifest more and more the divine consciousness contained in all forms. So, with each new form that it produces, Nature makes a form capable of expressing more completely the spirit which this form contains. But if it were like this, a form comes, develops, reaches its highest point and is followed by another form; the others do not disappear, but the individual does not progress. The individual dog or monkey, for instance, belongs to a species which has its own peculiar characteristics; when the monkey or the man arrives at the height of its possibilities, that is, when a human individual becomes the best type of humanity, it will be finished; the individual will not be able to progress any farther. He belongs to the human species, he will continue to belong to it. So, from the point of view of terrestrial history there is a progress, for each species represents a progress compared with the preceding species; but from the point of view of the individual, there is no progress: he is born, he follows his development, dies and disappears. Therefore, to ensure the progress of the individual, it was necessary to find another means; this one was not adequate. But within the individual, contained in each form, there is an organisation of consciousness which is closer to and more directly under the influence of the inner divine Presence, and the form which is under this influence — this kind of inner concentration of energy — has a life independent of the physical form — this is what we generally call the "soul" or the "psychic being" — and since it is organised around the divine centre it partakes of the divine nature which is immortal, eternal. The outer body falls away, and this remains throughout every experience that it has in each life, and there is a progress from life to life, and it is the progress of the *same* individual. And this movement complements the other, in the sense that instead of a species which progresses relative to other species, it is an individual who passes through all the stages of progress of these species and can continue to progress even when the species have reached the limit of their possibilities and... stay there or disappear — it depends on the case — but they cannot go any farther, whereas the individual, having a life independent of the purely material form, can pass from one form to another and continue his progress *indefinitely*. That makes a double movement which completes itself. And that is why each individual has the possibility of reaching the utmost realisation, independent of the form to which he momentarily belongs.

There are people — there used to be and there still are, I believe — who say they remember their past lives and recount what happened when they were dogs or elephants or monkeys, and tell you stories in great detail about what happened to them. I am not going to argue with them, but anyway this illustrates the fact that before being a man, one could have been a monkey — perhaps one doesn't have the power to remember it, that's another matter — but certainly, this inner divine spark has passed through successive forms in order to become more and more conscious of itself. And if it is proved that one can remember the form one had before becoming a psychic being as it is found in the human form, well, one might very well recollect climbing trees and eating coconuts and even playing all sorts of tricks on the traveller passing beneath!

In any case, the fact is there. Perhaps later we shall see that a certain state of inner organisation is necessary for this psychic being to be able to have memories in the way the mental being has them — we shall speak about it later, when we come to it in the book — but in any case the fact is established: it is this double movement of evolution intersecting and complementing itself which gives the utmost possibilities of realisation to the divine light within each being. This is what Sri Aurobindo has explained. (*Turning to the child*) This means that in your outer body you belong to the animal species in the course of becoming a supramental species — you are not that yet! but within you there's a psychic being which has already lived in many, many, countless species before and carries an experience of thousands of years within you, and which will continue while your human body remains human and finally decomposes.

We shall see later whether this psychic being has the possibility of transforming its body and itself creating an intermediate species between the animal man and superman — we shall study this later — but still, for the moment, it is an immortal soul which becomes more and more conscious of itself in the body of man. There. Now have you understood?

(Another child) *Mother, in Nature we often see the disappearance of an entire species. What is that due to?*

Probably Nature thought that it was not a success!... You see, she throws herself into action with abundance and a total lack of sense of economy. We can see this. She tries everything she can, in every way she can, with all sorts of inventions which are obviously very remarkable, but at times... it's like a blind alley. Pushing forward in that direction, instead of progressing, one would reach things that are absolutely unacceptable.

She throws out her creative spirit in an abundance without any calculation, and when the combination is not very successful, well, she just does this (*gesture*) then rejects it; she doesn't mind. For Nature, you see, there is a limitless abundance. I believe she doesn't shrink from any kind of experiment. Only if something has a chance of leading to a successful issue does it continue. Certainly there have been intermediaries or parallel forms between the ape and man; traces of them have been found — perhaps with some wishful thinking! but anyway, traces have been found — well, those species have disappeared. So, if we like to speculate, we may wonder whether the species which is now to come and which is an intermediary between animal man and superman will remain or whether it will be considered uninteresting and rejected.... That we shall see later. The next time we meet we shall speak about it again!

It is quite simply the activity of a limitless abundance. Nature has enough knowledge and consciousness to act like someone with innumerable and countless elements which can be mixed, separated again, reshaped, taken to pieces once more and... It is a huge cauldron: you stir it, and something comes out; it's no good, you throw it back in and take something else. Imagine the dimension... just take the earth: you understand, one or two forms or a hundred, for her this is of no importance at all, there are thousands and thousands and thousands of them; and then a few years, a hundred, a thousand, millions of years, it is of no importance at all, you have eternity before you!

Simply, when we look at things on the human scale, in space and time, oh! it seems enormous, but for Nature it is nothing. It is just a pastime. One may like it or not, this pastime, but still it is a pastime.

It is quite obvious that Nature enjoys it and is in no hurry. If she is told to press on without stopping and to finish one part of her work or another quickly, the reply is always the same: "But what for, why? Doesn't it amuse you?"

13 November 1957

> *I have a question about the first page where Sri Aurobindo says, "A spiritual evolution, an evolution of consciousness in Matter in a constant developing self-formation till the form can reveal the indwelling Spirit, is then the key-note, the central significant motive of the terrestrial existence."*
>
> The Life Divine, SABCL, Vol. 19, p. 824
>
> *So, from the point of view of form, in what way is man superior to other animals?*

I think this is quite easy to find.

Sri Aurobindo speaks of the form that is capable of manifesting the Spirit. The very nature of the manifestation of the Spirit is consciousness, understanding and finally mastery. It is obvious that from the point of view of aesthetics and purely physical appearance, one may find certain animal forms beautiful and perhaps even more beautiful than the human form in its present state of... degeneration, I believe. There were periods when the human race seems to have been more beautiful and harmonious; but as a means of expression of the Spirit, its superiority is beyond the shadow of a doubt. For the mere fact that man stands upright is symbolic of the capacity to look at things from above. He dominates what he sees instead of always having his nose to the ground. Of course, it may be said that birds fly, but with wings it is difficult to have a means of intellectual self-expression!

This upright position is very symbolic. If you try to walk on all fours, you will see that this position with the eyes and nose necessarily turned to the ground does not give you the feeling that you are looking at things from another plane or even from above. The whole structure of the human body is made to express a mental life. The proportions of the brain, for instance, the structure of the human head, the structure of the arms and hands, all that, from the point of view of the expression of the Spirit, is unquestionably altogether superior and it seems to have been conceived and built exclusively *for the purpose of* expressing intelligence.

Certainly from the point of view of strength, of suppleness, of agility, man is not the most gifted of animals, but for expressing the Spirit no other animal can be compared with him. Everything is made with this in view. We may wish to add to this possibility other things which seem to have been sacrificed just for the sake of the mental life — but also precisely because of this capacity of expressing a mental life man is able to develop in himself faculties which are only latent. Man has a power to educate: his body can be developed, educated. He can increase certain faculties. You cannot imagine any animal, even among those we most admire, which is capable, for instance, of physical education, purely physical — I am not speaking of going to school or learning things, but purely physical education, a systematic development of the muscles. The animal is born and makes good use of what it has and it grows according to its own law, but it does not educate itself or does it in a very rudimentary way, in an extremely limited field; whereas by a normal and systematic development man can remedy his defects and shortcomings. Man is certainly, in an organised way, the first progressive animal who can augment his capacities, his possibilities, increase his faculties and acquire things that he did not have spontaneously. There is not one animal which can do that.

Yes, under man's influence some animals have learnt movements they did not make spontaneously, but that is still under man's influence. Certainly without men dogs or horses would never have learnt to do what they have learnt through contact with man. So, it is obvious that the human physical form is the most appropriate one for expressing the Spirit. It may seem inadequate to us, but precisely we feel we are capable of drawing out from our bodies more than they would have given spontaneously without an educating will. And with this possibility of expressing intelligence, observation, comprehension, deduction — all the mental qualities — man has gradually learnt to understand the laws of Nature and tried not only to understand them but master them.

If we compare what he is with the higher being living in the Truth which we want to become, we may obviously speak about man as he is at present in a very derogatory fashion and complain of his imperfection. But if we put ourselves in the place of the animals which immediately precede him in the evolution, we see that

On "Man and the Evolution"

he is endowed with possibilities and powers which the others are quite incapable of expressing. The mere fact of having the ambition, the desire, the will to know the laws of Nature and to master them sufficiently to be able to adapt them to his needs and change them to a certain extent, is something impossible, unthinkable for any animal.

You may tell me that I don't usually speak very kindly about man (*laughter*), but that's because he usually thinks too kindly of himself!

If we compare him with the other products of Nature, unquestionably he is at the top of the ladder.

But, Mother, then the question arises: Does the descent of the consciousness develop the form or is it the development of the form that compels the descent of a higher consciousness?

There would be no universe without the descent of consciousness. Where would your universe begin, and with what?

In the case of man, did the animal man bring down the mind or was it the descent of mind...

Oh! You mean: Is it something in the intermediary being or in the higher ape which by its aspiration called down the mind? But the aspiration itself is the result of a previous descent.

It is quite obvious that nothing can be manifested

which is not previously contained in what exists. One can't bring something out of nothing. One can make what is there emerge, manifest, express itself, develop; but if nothing had been there, nothing would ever have come out. All progress, all perfection is the result of an inner effort of "something" that is present and seeks to manifest. That is to say, absolutely, the principle comes first and the expression afterwards. As we go on reading *The Life Divine*, Sri Aurobindo will prove this to you in every possible way. If there were not an eternal principle, if there were not — we give it all the names we like, can't we? — a Supreme Reality, there would never have been a universe, because nothing comes out of nothing.

We shall see this as we read on; then you will have to do philosophical gymnastics. But anyway, even without philosophy and mental gymnastics, it is obvious that to make something, you need to have something to make it with.

There is or was a whole period in the development of the human mind in which men tried very seriously to prove that it was the perfecting of Matter which produced the Spirit. But that is nonsense! (*Mother laughs*) The least of your activities, all that you do, is a clear proof that first you conceive and then you do, even on a very small scale. A life which is not the result of a conscious will would be a completely incoherent life. I mean that if Nature were not a conscious force and a conscious will with a conscious aim, nothing could ever have been organised. We have just to observe a little, even in the very small field of observation we have in our individual life, to be completely convinced of it.

But anyway... It is precisely one of the subjects Sri Aurobindo deals with in great detail, so we shall speak about it again.

(*Silence*)

It could be said that the mastery of fire is the symbolic sign of human superiority. Wherever there is man, a fire is lit.

The two things that are clearly superior to animal activities are the faculty of writing and the possibility of articulate speech. And this is something so clearly superior that all sufficiently developed animals are extremely sensitive to articulate speech; it fascinates them. If you speak in a very clear, very modulated, very well articulated way to a wild animal, it is immediately attracted, truly fascinated — I am not speaking of those which have lived close to man, but precisely of animals which have never met man before. They listen immediately, they feel the superior power that is being expressed.

27 November 1957

"It is open also to doubt whether the evolution is likely to go any farther than it has gone already or whether a supramental evolution, the appearance of a consummated Truth-Consciousness, a being of Knowledge, is at all probable in the fundamental Ignorance of the earthly Nature....

Admitting that the creation is a manifestation of the Timeless Eternal in a Time Eternity, admitting that there are the seven grades of Consciousness and that the material Inconscience has been laid down as a basis for the reascent of the Spirit, admitting that rebirth is a fact, a part of the terrestrial order, still a spiritual evolution of the individual being is not an inevitable consequence of any of these admissions or even of all of them together. It is possible to take another view of the spiritual significance and the inner process of terrestrial existence. If each thing created is a form of the manifest Divine Existence, each is divine in itself by the spiritual presence within it, whatever its appearance, its figure or character in Nature. In each form of manifestation the Divine takes the delight of existence and there is no need of change or progress within it. Whatever ordered display or hierarchy of actualised possibilities is necessitated by the nature of the Infinite Being, is sufficiently provided for by the numberless variation, the teeming multitude of forms, types of consciousness,

> *natures that we see everywhere around us. There is no teleological purpose in creation and there cannot be, for all is there in the Infinite: the Divine has nothing that he needs to gain or that he has not; if there is creation and manifestation, it is for the delight of creation, of manifestation, not for any purpose. There is then no reason for an evolutionary movement with a culmination to be reached or an aim to be worked out and effectuated or a drive towards ultimate perfection."*
>
> The Life Divine, SABCL, Vol. 19, pp. 826-27

This is an argument Sri Aurobindo is presenting. As he has said, it is *one* way of looking at the problem and solving it, but that does not mean that this is his own point of view. And this is exactly what he does throughout the book, all the time; he presents different arguments, different points of view, different conceptions, and once he has placed all these problems before us, then he comes and gives the solution. And that is why our method of reading has a drawback, for I read one paragraph to you and if we stop there, it seems as though he had proved his own point of view; and then, if by chance one doesn't remember very well and the next time I read another paragraph in which he expounds another point of view — sometimes totally different, sometimes even opposite — and we stop there, the conclusion is: this too is his point of view. So there is a contradiction. And then if we continue, there are two or three contradictions! I am telling you this because I have heard people who read in a rather superficial way and perhaps also don't read continuously enough — people who consider themselves extremely intelligent and learned — who have told me, "But Sri Aurobindo repeats himself all the time in this book! He tells us the same thing again in almost every paragraph." (*Mother laughs*) For he presents all other points of view, then gives his own, the conclusion; then once again he presents every point of view, gives all the problems, and ends up by proving the truth of what he wants to teach us — so he "repeats himself"!

After all, of course, one has only to read attentively enough to avoid falling into this trap. One must be careful, not come to a conclusion in the middle of a subject, not say to oneself, "Ah, look! Sri Aurobindo says it is like that." He does not say it is "like that", he tells you there are *some people* who say it is like that. And he shows you the problem as it is presented by many people, and then once again the same problem as presented by other people; and only when he has finished explaining to us all the points of view does he give his own conclusion. And what is exceedingly interesting is that his conclusion is always a synthesis: all the other points of view find their place provided they are properly arranged. This excludes nothing, it combines everything and synthesises all points of view.

But as we have a lesson every three weeks, we have time (*laughing*) to forget all we have read before! I don't know if you can remember the problem that was set?... no?...

Is there or is there not an individual evolution?...

On "Man and the Evolution"

There is a universal evolution — Sri Aurobindo has shown this — but within this universal evolution, is there or is there not an individual evolution?... Now, he has given us one theory — which holds together perfectly, which is quite logical, you see — but in which it is not at all necessary to postulate an individual evolution. The whole universal plan is logical, can be logically proved, without introducing the necessity of an individual evolution.

But if we continue with patience, in a little while he will prove to us why and how this notion of individual evolution must be introduced into the system of explanation that will be chosen. But what I should like to know is whether this problem has any reality for you or not — whether it corresponds to something you understand or not. If you have followed that, it is possible to conceive of a progressive, evolving universe, in which the individual is not necessarily evolving individually...

I must ask you questions to find out whether you understand first of all the difference between universal and individual evolution, and how both can proceed.

How does Nature proceed in its universal evolution? I think, you have understood this, haven't you?

One dies and is born again.... Physically, isn't it that?

Yes, I am speaking of the outer world, the physical world as we see it.

One dies and is born...

No, that is something else. What you say — dying and being born again, dying and being reborn — that is the process of individual evolution, provided that something of the individual persists through life and death, for if he died entirely and disintegrated entirely, what could be reborn? Necessarily something must persist — persist through the rebirths — otherwise it is no longer the same person. If nothing persists, it is not the individual who progresses, it is Nature. Nature makes use of matter; with this matter she produces forms — I am telling you this in an oversimplified way, but still — she has at her disposal a mass of matter and she makes combinations; she makes a form, then this form develops, but it disintegrates, it does not persist as an individual element. Why doesn't it persist? Because Nature needs matter, substance to make other forms. So she unmakes what she has made, then out of this she makes something else, and she continues in this way, and this could go on indefinitely without the individual progressing: the whole progresses.

Supposing you have some plasticine — you know plasticine for modelling, don't you? Good. You make a form, then when you have finished, you don't like it, so you break it up and make it into a paste again and try another form. You have made some progress, you try, you arrange; you say, "That didn't work, I am going to try this", and your form is a little better but it is still not what you want; so once again you break it, put some water, make a paste and then begin another form. And you can go on indefinitely. It is always the same substance but not the same being, for each one of your forms has its own particular existence as a form, and the moment you break it, nothing is left.

You may try to perfect the same form or try other forms; you may try, for instance, to make a dog or a horse, and then if you have not succeeded, you may begin again and make another horse or dog, but you may also begin something else. If you build a house and don't like your house, you demolish it and build another on another model, but nothing is left of the first house except the memory, if you want to keep it. In the same way, Nature begins with completely unconscious and amorphous matter, then tries one form and another; only, instead of doing as we would, one thing at a time, she makes millions of them all at once. But it is simply a matter of scale, it is because Nature has more means at her disposal, that is all. But that does not necessarily imply that there is something permanent — like a principle of life or a principle of consciousness — which enters into a form and persists when this form is broken to enter into another. It could simply be as you with your plasticine: you make something, unmake it, make it again, unmake it again, indefinitely, and there is nothing left — as I said — except the memory of what was made before. But if we admit individual evolution, there is something permanent which passes from one form to another and, with each new form, makes a new progress and becomes capable of entering into a higher form, more and more, until this "something" becomes a perfectly conscious being at the end of the evolution. Then this being would have a personal evolution which would duplicate — it won't be independent but simultaneous — and complement the evolution of Nature or rather *make use of* the evolution of Nature as a field for its own individual evolution.... Do you catch it this time? Good!

What Sri Aurobindo has presented here is the explanation of a world which would function quite logically and comprehensibly without any need of an individual being passing from one form into another, without anything permanent which would be free from all destruction, all death, which would persist through all its forms and would itself have a personal, individual progression *parallel* to the evolution of Nature.... It is as though in the form you have made, at the centre there were a little precious stone which you had placed there and wanted to cover with successive forms. You transfer your little precious stone from one form to another — and the comparison is still incomplete, for the precious stone becomes more and more precious as it passes from one object to another — and it would be as though, by passing from one form to another, it became more and more luminous and pure, and more and more clear-cut in form.

There. Do you understand or not?

A little.

On "Man and the Evolution"

A little. Ah! That's already something.

So, to round it off, do you think there is an individual evolution or not?... Do you have any experience of it?... And how could you have the experience? That would become interesting. How can individual evolution be experienced apart from the collective evolution of Nature?

Can you give the answer?

Unless one is conscious of the principle that is eternal in oneself, how can one know whether...

Ah! Good, that's good. That is all right, but then it amounts to asking you if you are conscious of this eternal principle which is in your being!

(*Silence*)

Are you going to look and see if you can find it within you?

Why is it so hidden?

Perhaps simply because one does not give it enough attention! If one took the trouble to open the doors, perhaps one would find it.... It is obviously a gentleman who does not like — a gentleman or a lady or something, or anything — which does not like ostentation, does not force itself on your attention at the surface. But perhaps it is waiting for you to go in search of it? Perhaps it is sitting very quietly, at the very back of the house, and you must open the doors one after another.

I don't find that it is hidden. I find it visible everywhere, all the time, at every moment, in all things. Shall we look? Shall we go and look?

(Meditation)

4 December 1957

"In fact we see that the principles of creation are permanent and unchanging: each type of being remains itself and does not try nor has any need to become other than itself; granting that some types of existence disappear and others come into being, it is because the Consciousness-Force in the universe withdraws its life-delight from those that perish and turns to create others for its pleasure. But each type of life, while it lasts, has its own pattern and remains faithful with whatever minor variations to that pattern: it is bound to its own consciousness and cannot get away from it into other-consciousness; limited by its own nature, it cannot transgress these boundaries and pass into other-nature. If the Consciousness-Force of the Infinite has manifested Life after manifesting Matter and Mind after manifesting Life, it does not follow that it will proceed to manifest Supermind as the next terrestrial creation. For Mind and Supermind belong to quite different hemispheres, Mind to the lower status of the Ignorance, Supermind to the higher status of the Divine Knowledge. This world is a world of the Ignorance and intended to be that only; there need be no intention to bring down the powers of the higher hemisphere into the lower half of existence or to manifest their concealed presence there; for, if they are at all existent here, it is in an occult incommunicable immanence

> *and only to maintain the creation, not to perfect it. Man is the summit of this ignorant creation; he has reached the utmost consciousness and knowledge of which he is capable: if he tries to go farther, he will only revolve in larger cycles of his own mentality. For that is the curve of his existence here, a finite circling which carries the Mind in its revolutions and returns always to the point from which it started; Mind cannot go outside its own cycle, — all idea of a straight line of movement or of progress reaching infinitely upward or sidewise into the Infinite is a delusion. If the soul of man is to go beyond humanity, to reach either a supramental or a still higher status, it must pass out of this cosmic existence, either to a plane or world of Bliss and Knowledge or into the unmanifest Eternal and Infinite."*
>
> *The Life Divine*, SABCL, Vol. 19, pp. 827-28

In fact, you should do a little preparatory work and note down the new idea in each new paragraph, adding it to the preceding ideas so that at the end of the chapter you have the complete picture; for if you ask me a question now about what I have just read, this question may require an answer that is sometimes almost contradictory to what we have seen in the previous paragraph. That comes from his way of going about the proof. It is as though Sri Aurobindo were putting himself at the centre of a kind of sphere, at the centre of a wheel the spokes of which end in a circumference. And he always goes back to his starting-point and goes all the way out to the surface, and so on, which gives the impression that he repeats the same thing several times, but it is simply the exposition of the thought so that one can follow it. One must have a very clear memory for ideas to really understand what he says.

I am emphasising this because, unless you proceed systematically, you won't derive much benefit from this reading; it will appear to you like a maze where it is very difficult to find one's way.... All the ideas are joined at the centre, and at the circumference they go in altogether different directions.

Have you any questions this time?... No.

It is difficult, isn't it? I read and I see quite well that it is difficult to ask a question, for until one has come to the end of the proof, one doesn't know what he is leading up to or what he wants to teach; and at the same time, if one were to read the whole exposition, it would be impossible — unless one has a specially faithful memory — to recall all the points. Before reaching the end one would have forgotten what is written at the beginning! It would be rather interesting to take notes, brief notes, to try to summarise each paragraph in one or two key-ideas so as to be able to compare them.

(Silence)

Sri Aurobindo says here that each species is satisfied with the particular characteristics of that species, the principles of its structure, and does not try to transform or change itself into a new species. The dog remains satisfied with being a dog, the horse with being a horse and never tries, for instance, to become an elephant! Starting from this Sri Aurobindo asks the question: Will man remain satisfied with being man or will he awaken to the necessity of being something other than man, that is, a superman?

That is the summary of the paragraph.

But when one is used to such expositions, if one has a speculative mind, and one reads this, something in the being is not satisfied. That is to say, this concerns only the most external form, that kind of crust of the being, but within oneself one feels "something" which has, on the contrary, a sort of imperative tendency to go beyond that form. And this is what Sri Aurobindo wants to bring home to us.

I have seen pet animals which truly had a sort of inner need to become something other than what they were. I knew dogs which were like that, cats, horses and even birds like that. The outer form was inevitably what it was, but there was something living and perceptible in the animal which was making an obvious effort to achieve another expression, another form. And every man who has gone beyond the stage of the animal man and become the human man truly has what I might call an "incorrigible" need to be something other than this thoroughly unsatisfactory semi-animal — unsatisfactory in its expression, its means of expression and its means of life. So the problem is this: Will this imperious need be effective enough in its aspiration for the form itself, the species, to develop and transform itself, or will it be only

On "Man and the Evolution"

this thing, this imperishable consciousness in the being, which will leave this form when it perishes to enter into a higher form which, besides, as far as we can see now, does not yet exist?

And the problem before us is: How will this higher form be created? If we consider the problem, it becomes very interesting. Is it by some process which we have to imagine, that this form will gradually transform itself in order to create a new one, or is it by some other means, a means still unknown to us, that this new form will appear in the world?

That is, will there be a continuity or will there be a sudden appearance of something new? Will there be a progressive transition between what we now are and what our inner spirit aspires to become, or will there be a break, that is, shall we be obliged to drop this present human form and wait for the appearance of a new form — an appearance the process of which we do not foresee and which will have no relation with what we are now? Can we hope that this body which is our present means of earthly manifestation, will have the possibility of transforming itself progressively into something which will be able to express a higher life, or will it be necessary to give up this form entirely to enter into another which does not yet exist on Earth?

That is the problem. It is a very interesting problem.

If you will reflect on it, it will lead you to a little more light.

We can reflect on it just now.

(*Meditation*)

When this talk was first published,
Mother added the following remarks:

> Why not both?
> Both will be there at the same time; the one does not exclude the other.
>
> *Yes, but will one be transformed into the other?*
>
> One will be transformed and will be like a rough outline of the other. And the other, the perfect one, will appear when this one comes into being. For both have their beauty and their purpose, therefore they will both be there.
>
> The mind always tries to choose — but it's not like that. Even all that we can imagine is much less than what will be. Truly speaking, everyone who has an intense aspiration and an inner certitude will be called upon to realise it.
>
> Everywhere, in all the fields, always, eternally, everything will be possible. And everything that is possible, everything will exist at a given moment — a given moment that will be more or less delayed, but everything will exist.
>
> Just as all sorts of possibilities have been found between the animals and man, possibilities which have not remained, so there will be all sorts of possibilities: each individual will try in his own way. And all this together

will help to prepare the future realisation.

The question might be asked: Will the human species be like some species which have disappeared from the earth?... Certain species have disappeared from the earth — but not species which have lasted as long as the human species. I don't think so; and certainly not the species which had in them the seed of progress, this possibility of progress. Rather one has the impression that evolution will follow a curve which will draw closer and closer to a higher species and, maybe, everything that is still too close to the lower species will fall away, just as those species have.

We always forget that not only is everything possible — everything, even the most contradictory things — but all the possibilities have at least one moment of existence.

11 December 1957

"Even if it be discovered hereafter that under certain chemical or other conditions Life makes its appearance, all that will be established by this coincidence is that in certain physical circumstances Life manifests, not that certain chemical conditions are constituents of Life, are its elements or are the evolutionary cause of a transformation of inanimate into animate Matter. Here as elsewhere each grade of being exists in itself and by itself, is manifested according to its own character by its own proper energy, and the gradations above or below it are not origins and resultant sequences but only degrees in the continuous scale of earth-nature."

The Life Divine, SABCL, Vol. 19, p. 829

Sweet Mother, how did the first man appear?

Sri Aurobindo says here,[1] precisely, that if we take the scientific point of view, we see that theories follow one another with great instability, and seem more like a

---

1. "...if the facts with which Science deals are reliable, the generalisations it hazards are short-lived; it holds them for some decades or some centuries, then passes to another generalisation, another theory of things. This happens even in physical Science where the facts are solidly ascertainable and verifiable by experiment...."

The Life Divine, SABCL, Vol. 19, p. 828

kind of series of imaginations than things which can be proved — if one takes the purely materialist point of view. People believe that because it is a materialist point of view, it is the easiest to prove, but quite obviously it is the most difficult. If we take the occult standpoint, there have been traditions, based perhaps on certain memories, but as they are altogether beyond any material proof, this knowledge is considered to be even more problematic than scientific imaginations and deductions. For any inner logic, it is easier to understand and admit, but one has no more proof than one has material proof that there was one first man or that there were several first men or that there was something which was not yet a man but almost a man. These are speculations.

Traditions — which of course are only oral traditions and from the scientific point of view quite questionable, but which are based on individual memories — say that the first man or the first human pair or the first human individuals were materialised in accordance with an occult method, something like the one Sri Aurobindo foretells for the future supramental process; that is, that beings belonging to higher worlds have, by a process of concentration and materialisation, built or formed for themselves bodies of physical matter. It probably wasn't the lower species which progressively produced a body which became the first human body.

According to spiritual and occult knowledge, consciousness precedes form; consciousness by self-concentration produces its form; whereas, according to the materialist idea, it is form which precedes consciousness and makes it possible for consciousness to manifest. For those who have some knowledge of the invisible worlds and a direct perception of the play of forces, there is no possible doubt: it is *necessarily* consciousness which produces a form in order to manifest. Now, the way things are arranged on earth, it is quite certainly a consciousness of a higher order which penetrates a form and helps to transform it, so that this form may become — either immediately or through successive generations — capable of manifesting that consciousness. For those who have the inner vision and knowledge, this is absolutely beyond doubt. It is impossible for it to be otherwise. But those who start from the other end, from below, will not admit it — but all the same it is not for ignorance to dictate knowledge to wisdom! And yet, this is what it does at present. As it is easier to doubt than to know, the human mind is accustomed to doubt everything; that is its first movement, and of course that is why it knows nothing.

Conception precedes manifestation and expression, that is quite certain. And all those who have had a direct contact with the past have the memory of a kind of human prototype, far superior to mankind at present, who came on earth as an example and a promise of what humanity will be when it reaches its acme.

(Silence)

There is in life a certain tendency to imitate, a sort of effort to copy "something". One can find very striking examples of this in animal life — it even begins already in plant life, but in animal life it is very striking. One could give numerous examples. And so, in that sense, one might very well conceive of a sort of effort of animal life to attempt to copy, to imitate, to create some resemblance to this ideal type which would be manifested on earth by occult means, and it was probably through successive attempts, by a more and more successful effort that the first human types were produced.

18 December 1957

Mother reads a paragraph from *The Life Divine* SABCL, Vol. 19, p. 829).

The only really important thing modern science has discovered is that from the purely outer and physical point of view things are not what they seem to be. When you look at a body, a human being, an object, a landscape, you perceive these things with the help of your eyes, your touch, hearing and, for the details, smell and taste; well, science tells you: "All that is illusory, you don't see things at all as they are, you don't touch them as they really are, you don't smell them as they really are, you don't taste them as they really are. It is the structure of your organs which puts you in contact with these things in a particular way which is entirely superficial, external, illusory and unreal."

From the point of view of science, you are a mass of — not even of atoms — of something infinitely more imperceptible than an atom, which is in perpetual movement. There is absolutely nothing which is like a face, a nose, eyes, a mouth; it is only just an appearance. And scientists come to this conclusion — like the uncompromising spiritualists of the past — that the world is an illusion. That is a great discovery, very great.... One step more and they will enter into the Truth. So, when somebody comes and says, "But I *see* this, I *touch* it, I *feel* it, I am sure of it", from the scientific point of view it's

On "Man and the Evolution"

nonsense. This could be said only by someone who has never made a scientific study of things as they are. So, by diametrically opposite roads they have come to the same result: the world as you see it is an illusion.

Now what is the truth behind this? People who have sought spiritual knowledge tell you, "We have experienced it", but of course it is a purely subjective experience; there are as yet no grounds on which one can say absolutely that the experience is beyond question for everybody. Everyone's experience is beyond question for him. And if one takes it a little further...

In fact, the value of an experience or a discovery could perhaps be proved by the power it gives, the power to change these appearances and transform things, circumstances and the world as it appears to us, in accordance with the will that manifests through that experience. It seems to me that the most universal proof of the validity of an individual or collective experience would be its power to make things — these appearances that we call the world — different from what they are. From the subjective point of view, the effect of the experience on an individual consciousness is an undeniable proof; for one who attains bliss, sovereign peace, unchanging delight, the profound knowledge of things, it is more than proved. The effects on the outer form depend on many other things besides the experience itself — depend perhaps on the first cause of these experiences — but out of all this, one thing seems to be a proof which is accessible to other people as well as to the one who has the experience; it is the power over other people and things — which for the ordinary consciousness is "objective". For instance, if a person who has attained the state of consciousness I am speaking about, had the power of communicating it to others, it would be partially — only partially — a proof of the reality of his experiences; but further, if the state of consciousness in which he is — for instance, a state of perfect harmony — could create this harmony in the outer world, in what apparently is not harmony, it would be, I think, the proof most readily accepted, even by the materialist scientific mind. If these illusory appearances could be changed into something more beautiful, more harmonious, happier than the world we live in now, this would perhaps be an undeniable proof. And if we take it a little farther, if, as Sri Aurobindo promises us, the supramental force, consciousness and light transform this world and create a new race, then, just as the apes and animals — if they could speak — could not deny the existence of man, so too man would not be able to deny the existence of these new beings — provided that they are different enough from the human race for this difference to be perceptible even to the deceptive organs of man.

From these deductions it would seem that the most conclusive and obvious aspect and the one which will probably be the first to manifest — probably — will be the aspect of Power, rather than the aspect of Joy or of Truth. For a new race to be founded on earth, it would necessarily have to be protected from other earthly elements in order to be able to survive; and power is

On "Man and the Evolution"

protection — not an artificial power, external and false, but the true strength, the triumphant Will. It is therefore not impossible to think that the supramental action, even before being an action of harmonisation, illumination, joy and beauty, might be an action of power, to serve as a protection. Naturally, for this action of power to be truly effective, it would have to be founded on Knowledge and Truth and Love and Harmony; but these things could manifest, visibly, little by little, when the ground, so to say, has been prepared by the action of a sovereign Will and Power.

But for the least of these things to be possible, there must first be a basis of *perfect* balance, the balance given by a total absence of egoism, a perfect surrender to the Supreme, the true purity: identification with the Supreme. Without this basis of perfect balance, the supramental power is dangerous, and one must *on no account* seek it or want to pull it down, for even in an infinitesimal quantity it is so powerful and so formidable that it can unbalance the entire system.

Since I am speaking to you about it, I would like to recommend something to you. In your desire for progress and your aspiration for realisation, take great care not to attempt to pull the forces towards you. Give yourself, open yourself with as much disinterestedness as you can attain through a constant self-forgetfulness, increase your receptivity to the utmost, but never try to *pull* the Force towards you, for wanting to pull is already a dangerous egoism. You may aspire, you may open yourself, you may give yourself, but never seek to take. When things go wrong, people blame the Force, but it is not the Force that is responsible: it is ambition, egoism, ignorance and the weakness of the vessel.

Give yourself generously and with a perfect disinterestedness and from the deeper point of view nothing bad will ever happen to you. Try to take and you will be on the brink of the abyss.

1 January 1958

> *O Nature, material Mother,*
> *Thou hast said that thou wilt collaborate*
> *and there is no limit*
> *to the splendour of this collaboration.*
> New Year Message, 1 January 1958

Sweet Mother, will you explain the message for this year?

It is already written! The explanation has already been written, it is ready for the *Bulletin* of February 21.[1]

There is nothing to explain. It is an experience, something that happened, and when it happened I noted it down, and as it turned out, it occurred just at the moment when I remembered that I had to write something for the year — which was next year at that time, that is, the year which begins today. When I remembered that I had to write something — not because of that, but simultaneously — this experience came, and when I noted it down, I realised that it was... it was the message for this year!

(*Silence*)

---

1. The text of this explanation is given in an appendix to this talk.

I will tell you only one thing: you should not misinterpret the meaning of this experience and imagine that from now on everything is going to take place without any difficulties and always in a manner that favours our personal desires. It is not on this plane. It does not mean that when we do not want it to rain, it will not rain! that when we want something to happen in the world, it will happen immediately; that all difficulties will be done away with and everything will be as it is in fairy-tales. It is not that. It is something much deeper: Nature, in her play of forces, has accepted the new Force which has manifested and included it in her movements. And as always, the movements of Nature are on a scale which is infinitely beyond the human scale and not visible to an ordinary human consciousness. It is an inner, psychological possibility which has come into the world rather than a spectacular change in earthly events.

I am saying this because you might be tempted to believe that fairy-tales were going to be realised on earth. It is not yet time for that.

(*Silence*)

One must have much patience and a very wide and very complex vision to understand how things happen.

(*Silence*)

The miracles which take place are not what could be called story-book miracles, in the sense that they don't happen as in stories. They are visible only to a very deep vision of things — very deep, very comprehensive, very vast.

(Silence)

One must already be capable of following the methods and ways of the Grace in order to recognise its action. One must already be capable of not being blinded by appearances in order to see the deeper truth of things.

We could usefully, this evening, just take this resolution: to try throughout the year to do our best, so that the time may not pass in vain.

Appendix

*Explanation of the New Year Message
of 1 January 1958*

In the course of one of our classes[1] I spoke of the limitless abundance of Nature, the inexhaustible creatrix who takes the multitude of forms and mixes them together, separates them again and remoulds them, unmakes and destroys them, to move on to ever new combinations. It is a huge cauldron, I said: she stirs things inside and brings out something; it's no good, she throws it in again and takes something else.... One or two forms or a hundred have no importance for her, there are thousands and thousands of forms, and then as for years, a hundred years, a thousand, millions of years, it is of no importance, you have eternity before you! It is quite obvious that Nature enjoys all this and that she is not in a hurry. If she is told to rush rapidly through and finish this or that part of her work quickly, the reply is always the same: "But why should I do so, why? Doesn't it amuse you?"

The evening I told you about these things, I identified myself totally with Nature, I joined in her game. And this movement of identification provoked a response, a sort of new intimacy between Nature and myself, a long movement of a growing closeness which culminated in an experience which came on the eighth of November.

1. 30 October 1957.

Suddenly Nature understood. She understood that this new Consciousness which has just been born does not seek to reject her but wants to embrace her entirely, she understood that this new spirituality does not turn away from life, does not recoil in fear before the formidable amplitude of her movement, but wants on the contrary to integrate all its facets. She understood that the supramental consciousness is here not to diminish but to complete her.

Then from the supreme Reality came this order, "Awake, O Nature, to the joy of collaboration." And the whole of Nature suddenly rushed forward in a great surge of joy, saying, "I accept, I shall collaborate." And at the same time, there came a calm, an absolute tranquillity so that the bodily vessel could receive and contain, without breaking, without losing anything, the mighty flood of this Joy of Nature which rushed forward as in a movement of gratitude. She accepted, she saw with all eternity before her that this supramental consciousness was going to fulfil her more perfectly, give a still greater strength to her movement, a greater amplitude, more possibilities to her play.

And suddenly I heard, as if they came from all the corners of the earth, those great notes one sometimes hears in the subtle physical, a little like those of Beethoven's Concerto in D-major, which come in moments of great progress, as though fifty orchestras had burst forth all in unison, without a single false note, to express the joy of this new communion between Nature and Spirit, the meeting of old friends who come together again after having been separated for so long.

Then these words came, "O Nature, Material Mother, thou hast said that thou wilt collaborate and there is no limit to the splendour of this collaboration."

And the radiant felicity of this splendour was sensed in perfect peace.

That is how the message for the new year was born.

8 January 1958

Mother reads a paragraph from *The Life Divine*.

We have decided to read paragraph by paragraph so that we can go into certain detailed explanations, but this method has one drawback: as I have already told you, it is that Sri Aurobindo takes up all the theories and expounds them in all their details, with all their arguments, in order to show later what their defects are and their inability to solve the problem, and to present his own solution; but *(laughing)*, when we stop in the middle of an argument and take a single paragraph, if we read this paragraph without going on to the very end, we may very well imagine or believe that he is giving his own opinion.

In fact there are some unscrupulous people who have done that, and when they wanted to prove that their own theories were correct, they quoted paragraphs from Sri Aurobindo without saying what went before or what came after, in support of their own theory. They said, "You see, Sri Aurobindo in *The Life Divine* has written that." He has written that, but that does not mean that it was his own way of seeing. And now we are facing the same difficulty. For the last two lessons, I think, I have been reading the detailed demonstration of one of the modern theories of life, evolution, the purpose of existence — or the purposelessness of existence — and

Sri Aurobindo presents this in quite a... conclusive way, as if it were his own theory and own way of seeing. We stop in the middle and are left with a kind of uneasiness and the feeling, "But that is not what he told us! How is it that he is expounding that to us now?..." It is quite a big drawback. But if I were to read to you the whole argument, when we came to the end you wouldn't remember the beginning and you wouldn't be able to follow! So the best thing is to go on quietly, one paragraph at a time, trying to understand what he is saying, but without thinking that he wants to prove to us that it is true. He simply wants to expound the theories with everything that supports them, without telling us that this is the best way of seeing things.

In reality, you should take this reading as an opportunity to develop the philosophical mind in yourself and the capacity to arrange ideas in a logical order and establish an argument on a sound basis. You must take this like dumb-bell exercises for developing muscles: these are dumb-bell exercises for the mind to develop one's brain. And you must not jump to hasty conclusions. If we wait with patience, at the end of the chapter he will tell us — and tell us on a basis of irrefutable argument — why he has come to the conclusion he arrives at.

Now, if there is anything that gives rise to a question...

Not in the text, Mother.

Something else? What?

Mother, we sometimes have sudden ideas. Where do they come from and how do they work in the head?

Where do they come from? — From the mental atmosphere.

Why do they come?... Perhaps you meet them on your way as one meets a passer-by in a public square. Most often it is that; you are on a road where ideas are moving about and it so happens that you meet this particular one and it passes through your head. Obviously, those who are in the habit of meditating, of concentrating, and for whom intellectual problems have a very concrete and tangible reality, by concentrating their minds they attract associated ideas, and a "company of ideas" is formed which they organise so as to solve a problem or clarify the question they are considering. But for this, one must have the habit of mental concentration and precisely that philosophical mind I was speaking about, for which ideas are living entities with their own life, which are organised on the mental chessboard like pawns in a game of chess: one takes them, moves them, places them, organises them, one makes a coherent whole out of these ideas, which are individual, independent entities with affinities among themselves, and which organise themselves according to inner laws. But for this, one must also have the habit of meditation, reflection, analysis, deduction, mental organisation. Otherwise, if one is just "like that", if one lives life as it comes, then it is exactly like a public square: there are roads and on the roads people pass by, and then you find yourself at crossroads and it all passes through your head — sometimes even ideas without any connection between them, so much so that if you were to write down what passes through your head, it would make a string of admirable nonsense!

We once said that we could usefully try out a little game: to ask somebody suddenly, "What are you thinking about?" Well, it is not often that he can answer you clearly, "Ah! I was just thinking of that particular thing." If he says that, you may infer that he is a thoughtful person. Otherwise, the usual spontaneous reply is, "Oh! I don't know."

You see, all those who have done ordered and organised physical exercises, have the knowledge, for instance, of the various muscles which must be moved to obtain a particular movement, and the best way to move them and how to obtain the maximum result with the minimum loss of energy. Well, it is the same thing with thought. When you train yourself methodically, there comes a time when you can follow a train of reasoning quite objectively, as you would project a picture on a screen — you can follow the logical deduction of one idea from another, and the normal, logical, organised movement, with the minimum loss of time, from a proposition to its conclusion. Once you have acquired the habit of doing that, just as you have the habit of methodically moving the muscles which must be moved to obtain a certain result, your thought becomes clear. Otherwise, movements of thought, intellectual movements, are

On "Man and the Evolution" 57

vague, imprecise, elusive; all of a sudden something rises up, one doesn't know why, and something else comes to contradict it, one doesn't know why either. And if one tries to organise this clearly in order to become aware of the exact relation between ideas, the first few times one does it, one gets a fine headache! And one has the feeling of trying to find one's way in a very dark virgin forest.

The speculative mind needs discipline for its development. If it is not disciplined methodically, one is always in a sort of a cloud. The vast majority of human beings can harbour the most contradictory ideas in their brains without being in the least troubled by them.

Well, until you try to organise your mind clearly, you risk at the very least having no control over what you think. And very often, you must come down to action before you begin to realise the value of what you think! Or, if not as far as action, at least as far as the feelings: suddenly you become aware that you have feelings which are not very desirable; then you realise you have not controlled your way of thinking at all.

Sweet Mother, do people have bad thoughts because they have no control over their minds?

Bad thoughts?.... There can be several reasons for that. In fact there are several reasons. It may be due to a bad nature — if people have nasty feelings, these nasty feelings can be the cause of nasty thoughts. It may be the opposite. Perhaps they are wide open to all sorts of suggestions from outside and, as I said, these suggestions enter them and gradually create nasty feelings. It may be due to subconscious influences which are conflicting precisely because they are uncontrolled. When these influences rise to the surface, instead of being controlled and those which are undesirable refused, everything is allowed to enter as it likes, the doors are open.

You are *bathed* in all kinds of things — good, bad, neutral, luminous, dark; it's all there, and each one's consciousness should, in principle, act as a filter. You should receive only what you want to receive, you should think only what you want to think; and then, you should not allow these thoughts to be changed into feelings and actions without formal authorisation.

In fact, this is the very purpose of physical existence. Each person is an instrument for controlling a certain set of vibrations which represent his particular field of work; each one must receive only the ones which are in conformity with the divine plan and refuse the rest.

But not one in a thousand does that. You do it a little, half consciously, due to the friction of circumstances and surroundings, but as for doing it deliberately, surely there are very few human beings who do it deliberately; and even when it's done deliberately, to do it in the true way and with the true knowledge, that indeed is still more exceptional.

Thought-control! Who can control his thoughts? Only those who have trained themselves to it, who have tried hard since their childhood.

There is the whole range, you see, from total lack of control, which for most people comes to this: it is their

On "Man and the Evolution"

thoughts which rule them and not they their thoughts. The vast majority of people are troubled by thoughts they cannot get rid of, which literally possess them, and they don't have the power to close the door of their active consciousness to these thoughts. Their thoughts govern them, rule them. You hear people saying every day, "Oh! That thought, all the time it comes back to me, again and again, and I can't get rid of it!" So they are assailed by all kinds of things, from anxiety to ill-will and fear. Thoughts which express dread are extremely troublesome; you try to send them away, they return like a rubber band and fall back on you. Who has control? It requires years of labour and such a long practice. And so, to come to something which is not complete control but anyway already represents a stage: to have the ability to do this in your head (*Mother moves her hand across her brow*), to annul all the movements, to stop the vibrations. And the mental surface becomes smooth. Everything stops, as when you open a book at a blank page — but almost materially, you understand... blank!

Try a little when you are at home, you will see, it is very interesting.

And so, one follows the place in one's head where the little point is dancing. I have seen — I have seen Sri Aurobindo doing this in somebody's head, somebody who used to complain of being troubled by thoughts. It was as if his hand reached out and took hold of the little black dancing point and then did this (*gesture with the finger-tips*), as when one picks up an insect, and he threw it far away. And that was all. All still, quiet, luminous....

It was clearly visible like this, you know, he took it out without saying anything — and it was over.

And things are very closely interdependent: I also saw the case when someone came to him with an acute pain somewhere: "Oh, it hurts here! Oh, it hurts! Oh!..." He said nothing, he remained calm, he looked at the person, and I saw, I saw something like a subtle physical hand which came and took hold of the little point dancing about in disorder and confusion, and he took it like this (*same gesture*) and there, everything had gone.

"Oh, oh! look, my pain has gone."

There.

15 January 1958

Mother reads a paragraph from The Life Divine *continuing arguments from the point of view that each type of being, including man, is fixed in its type and does not progress, and that if a new creation is intended, it cannot develop out of man (SABCL, Vol. 19, p. 832).*

If all these arguments were true and there were to be no higher realisation... there would be nothing left to do. But fortunately this is not true.

Only, Sri Aurobindo has said many times that there will be no irrefutable proof of the truth of what he has said and predicted until it is accomplished; only when everything is accomplished will those who refuse to believe be obliged to recognise their mistake — but perhaps they won't be there to do it!

So there is only one thing to do: to proceed on one's way keeping one's own faith and certitude, and to pay no heed to contradictions and denials.

There are people who need the support and trust and certitude of others to feel comfortable and to be at ease — they are always unhappy because, of course, they will always come across people who do not believe, and so they will be upset and it will trouble them. One must find one's certitude within oneself, keep it in spite of everything and go one's way whatever the cost, to the very end. The Victory is for the most enduring.

To maintain one's endurance in spite of all oppositions, the support must be unshakable, and one support alone is unshakable, that of the Reality, the Supreme Truth.

It is useless to look for any other. This is the only one that never fails.

22 January 1958

> Mother reads a passage from *The Life Divine* which concludes the exposition of the intellectual arguments against the appearance of a higher species.

Next time we begin the argument. All these arguments take place in a field where you don't usually go, do you? It is a domain which is unfamiliar to you.

In fact it is a very special domain, far removed from action or any practical realisation. It has always seemed to me that one could take up any idea at all and use it as the starting-point for an argument and through intellectual logic succeed in proving that this idea is altogether true, simply by the power of argumentation.

It is quite remarkable that these are two fields of human activity — action and speculation — which usually find it difficult to be together at the same time in the consciousness; and it is even unusual that a man with a highly developed speculative mind should ever be a man of action, and on the other hand, that a man of action should ever feel at ease in the speculative intellect.

When one has an essentially practical bent for accomplishing things, one always feels that all these speculations, arguments, deductions are a more or less interesting occupation for idle people. But... I dare not say this too loud, for it is not appreciated by intellectuals, this has always seemed to me a gymnastic exercise that's very interesting from the point of view of mental development, but without much practical result. Now, if you listen to people with an abstract turn of mind, they will tell you that physical gymnastics are a thoroughly futile occupation without any practical result: "What's the use of doing gymnastics? It is simply to exercise your muscles. And why should we not exercise our mental muscles as you exercise the muscles of your body?" And both arguments are of equal value. For me the solution lies elsewhere.

(*Long silence*)

As soon as one is convinced that there is a living and real Truth seeking to express itself in an objective universe, the only thing that seems to have any importance or value is to come into contact with this Truth, to identify oneself with it as perfectly as possible, and to no longer be anything but a means of expressing it, making it more and more living and tangible so that it may be manifested more and more perfectly. All theories, all principles, all methods are more or less good according to their capacity to express that Truth; and as one goes forward on this path, if one goes beyond all the limits of the Ignorance, one becomes aware that the totality of this manifestation, its wholeness, its integrality is necessary for the expression of that Truth, that *nothing* can be left out, and perhaps that there is nothing more important or less important. The one thing that seems necessary is a harmonisation of everything which puts each thing in

On "Man and the Evolution"

its place, in its true relation with all the rest, so that the total Unity may manifest harmoniously.

If one comes down from this level, according to me one no longer understands anything and all arguments are of equal worth in the narrowness and limitation which take away all their real value.

Each thing in its place, in harmony with all the rest, and then one can begin to understand and to live.

(*Silence*)

One feels that a single movement, however small it may be, however insignificant it may seem, which is in harmony with that Truth, is of more value than the most wonderful arguments.

Let one single drop of light shine in you and it will be more effective in dissolving the darkness than the most beautiful speeches in the world on what light is or on what it can do.

29 January 1958

> *"Even in the Inconscient there seems to be at least an urge of inherent necessity producing the evolution of forms and in the forms a developing Consciousness, and it may well be held that this urge is the evolutionary will of a secret Conscious-Being and its push of progressive manifestation the evidence of an innate intention in the evolution.... Truth of Being inevitably fulfilling itself would be the fundamental fact of the evolution, but Will and its purpose must be there as part of the instrumentation, as an element in the operative principle."*
> The Life Divine, SABCL, Vol. 19, p. 834

Sweet Mother, I did not understand the last part of the sentence.

What don't you understand? He says that evolution is the result of the inevitable fulfilment of the Truth of Being which is the essential reality of the universe. The fulfilment of this Truth, the fulfilment of the Truth of Being, is the fundamental fact of evolution, that is, it is the cause and principle of the evolution; but naturally, if this Truth of Being is inevitably fulfilled, it must be by means of a will and a purpose. There has to be an aim and the will to fulfil that aim.

To fulfil itself this truth must contain a will to fulfilment and an aim, a purpose, a project it wants to fulfil.

On "Man and the Evolution"

In order to accomplish something, one must have the will to do it, and to have the will to do it, one must know what one wants to do. If one doesn't know what one wants to do, one can't do it. First one must *know*, have a plan, a purpose, a programme if you like; one must know what one wants to do, and then one must *will* to do it, and then one can do it.

You see, he says: the universe is the evolutionary fulfilment of the truth of the universal Being. The deploying of the universe is the progressive, evolutionary fulfilment of the truth of the universal Being, but for this truth to be fulfilled it must necessarily contain a plan, that is, it must know what it wants to do and must have the will to do it.

When you do something you know what you want to do, don't you? And then you will to do it, otherwise you couldn't. But it is the same thing, this is what he says.

It must necessarily be admitted that there is a plan in the universe, that it is not something that comes about by chance, and that there is a Will to fulfil this plan, otherwise nothing could happen. You see, Sri Aurobindo contradicts those who say that the universe has no plan and no will. But the minute we admit that there is a consciousness — a conscious existence — behind the universe, we admit at the same time, automatically, that there is a plan in this universe and a will to fulfil this plan. That is all he says. It is simple, isn't it?

You only have to reduce this to the individual scale. When someone is conscious and does something consciously, he necessarily does it knowing what he wants to do, with a plan. For instance, when you prepare a programme for the anniversary of your "boarding", you have a purpose, don't you? — you want to make a programme for the anniversary, and so you have a plan, you choose what you are going to enact and how it is going to be enacted, and at the same time you *want* to do it, otherwise you would not do it — so, Sri Aurobindo says just that. That is, that if the universe is a conscious entity, if there is a Consciousness which expresses itself, it necessarily expresses itself in accordance with a plan and with a will to express itself — it is quite simple.

Have you understood?... A little!

Don't you know this, that in order to do something one must know what one wants to do and then one must do it, have the will to do it? Even if you decide to walk from here to there, you must decide that you want to walk from here to there, and afterwards you must have the will to walk, otherwise you would not move. No?

Yes.

Ah! it is nothing but that, it is as simple as that.

(*Silence*)

People usually do things so automatically and spontaneously, without watching themselves doing them, that if they were to ask themselves how it comes about, they would require some time before the process becomes conscious to them. You are so used to living that you don't even know how it happens. All the gestures and movements of life are made spontaneously, automatically, almost unconsciously, in a semi-conscious state, and one doesn't even realise this very simple fact that in order to do something, one must first know what one is going to do and then must want to do it. It is only when something goes wrong with one of these elements — for instance, the ability to make a plan in one's mind and the ability to carry out this plan — when these two begin to go wrong, one starts worrying about whether one's being is in good order. For example, if one morning on waking up in bed you did not know or remember that you had to get up, wash and dress, have your breakfast, do this and that, you would say to yourself, "Why, what's the matter? Something is wrong — I don't know what I ought to do any more; something must be out of order."

And if, later, knowing what you have to do — you must get up, go for your bath, dress — you know you have to do it but you can't do it: there is something, the stimulus of the will, which is no longer working, has no effect on the body; then once again you begin to feel anxious, you say, "Well, well, could I be ill by any chance?" Otherwise you are not even aware that the whole of life is like that. It seems quite natural to you, it is "like that". That means that you act in a way which is hardly semi-conscious; it is automatic, it is a kind of spontaneous habit and you don't watch what you are doing. And so, if you want to have some control over your movements, the first thing is to know what is happening.

And in fact, this perhaps is the reason why things don't always go well. For if they went according to a normal, usual rhythm, one would never be conscious of what one is doing; one would do it by habit, automatically, spontaneously, without thinking, and would not watch what one is doing, and so one would never be able to acquire self-mastery. It would be "something", a vague consciousness in the background expressing itself without your even watching what you are doing, and which would make you act; and then if there came along some strange or unknown current of force, it could make you do anything at all, without your even noticing the process by which it makes you act. And in fact that is what does happen.

It is only when one is fully conscious of the process, when one knows how life works, the movement of life and the process of life, that one can begin to have control; otherwise at first one doesn't even think at all of having any control; but if unpleasant things occur, if, for instance, you do something which has unfortunate consequences and you tell yourself, "Oh! But I should stop doing that", then, at that moment, you realise that there is a whole technique of "how to live" which is necessary to be able to control your life! Otherwise one is a kind of more or less coordinated medley of actions and reactions, of movements and impulses, and one doesn't know at all how things happen. This is what is developed in the being by shocks, frictions, all the apparent disorders of life, and what forms the consciousness in very small children. A small child is altogether unconscious, and only gradually, very gradually, does he begin to grow aware of things. But unless they take special care, people live almost their whole life without even knowing how they do it! They are not aware of it.

So anything at all can happen.

But that is the very *first little* step towards becoming conscious of oneself in the material world.

You have vague thoughts and feelings, don't you, which develop more or less logically in the being — rather less than more — then you have a faint impression of that; and again, when you get burnt, you realise that something is wrong, when you fall and hurt yourself, you realise that something is wrong: it begins to make you reflect that you must pay attention to this and that, so as not to fall, not to burn yourself, not to cut yourself.... It dawns on you gradually with external experience, external contacts. But otherwise one is a half-conscious mass which moves without even knowing why or how.

This is the very small beginning of the emergence from the primary state of unconsciousness.

5 February 1958

> "*The metaphysical objection [to a teleological cosmos] is more serious; for it seems self-evident that the Absolute can have no purpose in manifestation except the delight of manifestation itself: an evolutionary movement in Matter as part of the manifestation must fall within this universal statement; it can be there only for the delight of the unfolding, the progressive execution, the objectless seried self-revelation. A universal totality may also be considered as something complete in itself; as a totality, it has nothing to gain or to add to its fullness of being. But here the material world is not an integral totality, it is part of a whole, a grade in a gradation; it may admit in it, therefore, not only the presence of undeveloped immaterial principles or powers belonging to the whole that are involved within its Matter, but also a descent into it of the same powers from the higher gradations of the system to deliver their kindred movements here from the strictness of a material limitation. A manifestation of the greater powers of Existence till the whole being itself is manifest in the material world in the terms of a higher, a spiritual creation, may be considered as the teleology of the evolution. This teleology does not bring in any factor that does not belong to the totality; it proposes only the realisation of the totality in the part. There can be no objection to the admission*

of a teleological factor in a part movement of the universal totality, if the purpose, — not a purpose in the human sense, but the urge of an intrinsic Truth-necessity conscious in the will of the indwelling Spirit, — is the perfect manifestation there of all the possibilities inherent in the total movement. All exists here, no doubt, for the delight of existence, all is a game or Lila; but a game too carries within itself an object to be accomplished and without the fulfilment of that object would have no completeness of significance. A drama without denouement may be an artistic possibility, — existing only for the pleasure of watching the characters and the pleasure in problems posed without a solution or with a forever suspended dubious balance of solution; the drama of the earth evolution might conceivably be of that character, but an intended or inherently predetermined denouement is also and more convincingly possible. Ananda is the secret principle of all being and the support of all activity of being: but Ananda does not exclude a delight in the working out of a Truth inherent in being, immanent in the Force or Will of being, upheld in the hidden self-awareness of its Consciousness-Force which is the dynamic and executive agent of all its activities and the knower of their significance."

The Life Divine, SABCL, Vol. 19, pp. 834-35

If one wants to state the problem in a way that's more easily accessible to ordinary practical thinking, one could conceive that everything exists from all eternity, and therefore simultaneously, but that this total, simultaneous, eternal existence is like the property, the possession of a Consciousness which would take pleasure in travelling through its domains, find its joy in an almost infinite or anyway indefinite journey throughout all its domains, and would go like this from discovery to discovery of things which already exist, which have always existed... but which the Supreme had never visited. And the path he follows in his discovery could be an entirely free, unexpected, unforeseen path according to his choice of the moment, so that, although his whole domain is there from all eternity, existing for ever, he could visit it in an altogether unexpected, unpredictable way, and so open the door to all relationships and possibilities.

And it is also his own self-discovery, for this domain is himself; and a discovery which could be made according to immediate decisions, without a preconceived plan such as would be mentally thought out, with all the delight of complete freedom and of the unexpectedness of every second — an eternal journey within his own being.

Everything is absolutely determined, for everything is from all eternity, and yet the path traversed has a freedom and unpredictability which is also absolute.

And this is how there can exist simultaneously worlds which have no apparent relationship with each other, and which nevertheless coexist, but are discovered gradually and so give the impression of a new creation.... Seeing things in this way, one could easily

On "Man and the Evolution"

understand that simultaneously with this physical world as we know it with all its imperfections, all its limitations, all its ignorance, there are one or several other worlds which exist in their own zones and are so different in nature from ours here, that for us they are as if non-existent, for we have no relation with them. But the moment the great eternal Voyage passes from this world to that, by the very fact of this passage of the eternal Consciousness, the link will necessarily be created, and the two worlds will gradually enter into relation with each other.

Truly speaking this is what is actually happening, and we can say with certainty that the supramental world already exists, but the time has come for it to become the object of the journey of the supreme Consciousness, and then, gradually, a conscious link will be formed between this world and that, and they will have a new relation as a result of this new orientation of the journey.

This explanation is as good as any other and perhaps it is easier to understand for people who are not metaphysicians.... At least, I like it!

Mother, you said that everything was absolutely determined; then where does personal effort come from?

I told you just a moment ago that the Great Traveller chooses at each instant the course of his journey, therefore it is an absolute freedom of choice, and this is what gives the universal unfolding that unpredictable air and that possibility of change, for the Supreme is entirely free to change his course if he wants to do so. On the contrary, this is absolute freedom. But everything is there, and since everything is there, everything is absolutely determined — it has always existed but it is discovered in an altogether unforeseen way. And in this discovery lies freedom.

You are taking a walk and, suddenly, well, you feel like going this way instead of that, so the course you take is completely new, but in the places you are going to, the things were already there, they existed and were therefore determined — but not your discovery.

Surely only a consciousness identified with the supreme Consciousness can have this feeling of absolute freedom. So long as you are not one with the supreme Consciousness, you necessarily have the impression or the feeling or idea that you are subject to the law of a higher Will, but the moment you are identified with this Will you are perfectly free. This amounts to saying what Sri Aurobindo has always said: in union with the Supreme true freedom is realised.

12 February 1958

Mother, since in each new life the mind and vital as well as the body are new, how can the experiences of past lives be useful for them? Do we have to go through all the experiences once again?

That depends on people!

It is not the mind and vital which develop and progress from life to life — except in altogether exceptional cases and at a very advanced stage of evolution — it is the psychic. So, this is what happens: the psychic has alternate periods of activity and rest; it has a life of progress resulting from experiences of the physical life, of active life in a physical body, with all the experiences of the body, the vital and the mind; then, normally, the psychic goes into a kind of rest for assimilation where the result of the progress accomplished during its active existence is worked out, and when this assimilation is finished, when it has absorbed the progress it had prepared in its active life on earth, it comes down again in a new body bringing with it the result of all its progress and, at an advanced stage, it even chooses the environment and the kind of body and the kind of life in which it will live to complete its experience concerning one point or another. In some very advanced cases the psychic can, before leaving the body, decide what kind of life it will have in its next incarnation.

When it has become an almost completely formed

and already very conscious being, it presides over the formation of the new body, and usually through an inner influence it chooses the elements and the substance which will form its body in such a way that the body is adapted to the needs of its new experience. But this is at a rather advanced stage. And later, when it is fully formed and returns to earth with the idea of service, of collective help and participation in the divine Work, then it is able to bring to the body in formation certain elements of the mind and vital from previous lives which, having been organised and impregnated with psychic forces in previous lives, could be preserved and, consequently, can participate in the general progress. But this is at a very, very advanced stage.

When the psychic is fully developed and very conscious, when it becomes a conscious instrument of the divine Will, it organises the vital and the mind in such a way that they too participate in the general harmony and can be preserved.

A high degree of development allows at least some parts of the mental and vital beings to be preserved in spite of the dissolution of the body. If, for instance, some parts — mental or vital — of the human activity have been particularly developed, these elements of the mind and vital are maintained even "in their form" — in the form of the activity which has been fully organised — as, for example, in highly intellectual people who have particularly developed their brains, the mental part of their being keeps this structure and is preserved in the form of an organised brain which has its own life and can be kept unchanged until a future life so as to participate in it with all its gains.

In artists, as for instance in certain musicians who have used their hands in a particularly conscious way, the vital and mental substance is preserved in the form of hands, and these hands remain fully conscious, they can even use the body of living people if there is a special affinity — and so on.

Otherwise, in ordinary people in whom the psychic form is not fully developed and organised, when the psychic leaves the body, the mental and vital forms may persist for a certain time if the death has been particularly peaceful and concentrated, but if a man dies suddenly and in a state of passion, with numerous attachments, well, the different parts of the being are dispersed and live for a shorter or longer time their own life in their own domain, then disappear.

The centre of organisation and transformation is always the presence of the psychic in the body. Therefore, it is a very big mistake to believe that the progress continues or even, as some believe, that it is more complete and rapid in the periods of transition between two physical lives; in general, there is no progress at all, for the psychic enters into a state of rest and the other parts, after a more or less ephemeral life in their own domain, are dissolved.

Earthly life is the place for progress. It is here, on earth, that progress is possible, during the period of earthly existence. And it is the psychic which carries the progress over from one life to another, by organising its own evolution and development itself.

19 February 1958

Mother reads her comments upon an experience she had on February 3:

Between the beings of the supramental world and men, almost the same separation exists as between men and animals. Some time ago I had the experience of identification with animal life, and it is a fact that animals do not understand us; their consciousness is so constructed that we elude them almost entirely. And yet I have known pet animals — cats and dogs, but especially cats — that used to make an almost yogic effort of consciousness to reach us. But usually, when they see us as we live and act, they do not understand, they do not see us as we are and they suffer because of us. We are a constant enigma to them. Only a very tiny part of their consciousness has a link with us. And it is the same thing for us when we try to look at the supramental world. Only when the link of consciousness is established shall we see it — and even then only the part of our being which has undergone transformation in this way will be able to see it as it is — otherwise the two worlds would remain apart like the animal and human worlds.

The experience I had on the third of February is a proof of this. Before that I had had an individual subjective contact with the supramental world, whereas on the third of February I moved in it concretely, as concretely as I once used to walk in Paris, in a world *that exists in itself*, outside all subjectivity. It is like a bridge being thrown between the two worlds. Here is the experience as I dictated it immediately afterwards:

(*Silence*)

The supramental world exists permanently and I am there permanently in a supramental body. I had the proof of this even today when my earth-consciousness went there and remained there consciously between two and three o'clock in the afternoon. Now, I know that what is lacking for the two worlds to unite in a constant and conscious relation, is an intermediate zone between the physical world as it is and the supramental world as it is. This zone remains to be built, both in the individual consciousness and the objective world, and it is being built. When I used to speak of the new world which is being created, it was of this intermediary zone that I was speaking. And similarly, when I am on this side, that is, in the field of the physical consciousness, and I see the supramental power, the supramental light and substance constantly penetrating matter, it is the construction of this zone which I see and in which I participate.

I was on a huge boat which was a symbolic representation of the place where this work is going on. This boat, as large as a city, is fully organised, and it had certainly already been functioning for some time, for its organisation was complete. It is the place where people who are destined for the supramental life are trained. These people — or at least a part of their being — had already undergone a supramental transformation, for the boat itself and everything on board was neither material nor subtle-physical nor vital nor mental — it was a supramental substance. This substance was of the most material supramental, the supramental substance which is closest to the physical world, the first to manifest. The light was a mixture of gold and red, forming a uniform substance of a luminous orange. Everything was like that — the light was like that, the people were like that — everything had that colour, although with various shades which made it possible to distinguish things from each other. The general impression was of a world without shadows; there were shades but no shadows. The atmosphere was full of joy, calm, order; everything went on regularly and in silence. And at the same time one could see all the details of an education, a training in all fields, by which the people on board were being prepared.

This immense ship had just reached the shore of the supramental world and a first group of people who were destined to become the future inhabitants of this supramental world were to disembark. Everything had been arranged for this first landing. At the wharf several very tall beings were posted. They were not human beings, they had never been men before. Nor were they the permanent inhabitants of the supramental world. They had been delegated from above and posted there to control and supervise the landing. I was in charge of the whole thing from the beginning and all the time. I had prepared all the groups myself. I stood on the boat at the head of the gangway, calling the groups one by one and sending them down to the shore. The tall beings who were posted there were inspecting, so to say, those who were landing, authorising those who were ready and sending back those who were not and who had to continue their training on board the ship. While I was there looking at everybody, the part of my consciousness which came from here became extremely interested; it wanted to see and recognise all the people, see how they had changed and check which ones were taken immediately and which ones had to remain to continue their training. After a while, as I stood there observing, I began to feel that I was being pulled back so that my body might wake up — a consciousness or a person here — and in my consciousness I protested, "No, no, not yet, not yet! I want to see the people!" I was seeing and noting everything with intense interest.... Things continued in this way until suddenly the clock here began to strike three, and this brought me back violently. There was a sensation of suddenly falling into my body. I came back with a shock because I had been called back very suddenly, but with all my memory. I remained quiet, without moving, until I could recollect the whole experience and keep it.

On the boat the nature of objects was not the one we know on earth; for instance, clothes were not made of cloth and what looked like cloth was not manufactured: it formed a part of the body, it was made of the same substance which took different forms. It had a kind of plasticity. When a change had to be made, it took place, not by any artificial and external means but by an inner operation, an operation of consciousness which gave form or appearance to the substance. Life created its own forms. There was *one single* substance in everything; it changed the quality of its vibration according to need and use.

Those who were sent back for fresh training were not of a uniform colour, it was as if their body had greyish, opaque patches of a substance resembling earthly substance; they were dull, as if they had not been entirely permeated with light, not transformed. They were not like that everywhere, only in places.

The tall beings on the shore were not of the same colour, at least they did not have that orange tint; they were paler, more transparent. Except for one part of their body, one could only see the outline of their form. They were very tall, they seemed not to have any bones and could take any form according to their need. Only from the waist down had they a permanent density, which was not perceptible in the rest of their body. Their colour was much lighter, with very little red, it was more golden or even white. The parts of whitish light were translucent; they were not positively transparent but less dense, more subtle than the orange substance.

When I was called back and while I was saying "Not yet", each time I had a brief glimpse of myself, that is, of my form in the supramental world. I was a mixture of the tall beings and the beings aboard the ship. My upper part, particularly the head, was only a silhouette whose contents were white with an orange fringe. Going down towards the feet, the colour became more like that of the people on the boat, that is, orange; going upwards, it was more translucent and white and the red grew less. The head was only a silhouette with a sun shining within it; rays of light came from it which were the action of the will.

As for the people I saw on board the ship, I recognised them all. Some were from here, from the Ashram, some came from elsewhere, but I know them too. I saw everybody but as I knew that I would not remember them all when I returned, I decided not to give any names. Besides, it is not necessary. Three or four faces were very clearly visible, and when I saw them, I understood the feeling I had here on earth when looking into their eyes: there was such an extraordinary joy.... People were mostly young, there were very few children and they were about fourteen or fifteen, certainly not below ten or twelve — I did not remain long enough to see all the details. There weren't any very old people, apart from a few exceptions. Most of the people who went ashore were middle-aged, except a few. Already, before this experience, some individual cases had been examined several times at a place where people capable of being supramentalised were examined; I had a few surprises and noted them; I even told some people about it. But the ones whom I put ashore today, I saw very distinctly; they were middle-aged, neither young children nor old people, apart from a few rare exceptions, and that corresponded fairly well with what I expected. I decided not to say anything, not to give any names. As I did not remain until the end, it was not possible for me to get an exact picture; the picture was not absolutely clear or complete. I do not want to say things to some and not to others.

What I can say is that the point of view, the judgment, was based *exclusively* on the substance of which the people were made, that is, whether they belonged completely to the supramental world, whether they were made of that very special substance. The standpoint taken is neither moral nor psychological. It is probable that the substance their bodies were made of was the result of an inner law or inner movement which at that time was not in question. At least it is quite clear that the values are different.

When I came back, simultaneously with the recollection of the experience I knew that the supramental world is permanent, that my presence there is permanent, and that only a missing link was necessary for the connection to be made in the consciousness and the substance, and it is this link which is now being forged. I had the impression — an impression which remained for quite a long time, almost a whole day — of an extreme relativity — no, not exactly that: the impression that the relation between this world and the other completely changed the standpoint from which things should be evaluated or appraised. This standpoint had nothing mental about it and it gave a strange inner feeling that lots of things we consider good or bad are not really so. It was very clear that everything depended on the capacity of things, on their aptitude in expressing the supramental world or being in relation with it. It was so completely different, sometimes even altogether contrary to our ordinary appraisal. I recollect one little thing which we usually consider to be bad; how strange it was to see that in truth it was something excellent! And other things we consider to be important have in fact absolutely no importance at all: whether a thing is like this or like that is not at all important. What is very obvious is that our appraisal of what is divine or undivine is not right. I even laughed to see certain things.... Our usual feeling of what is antidivine seems artificial, seems based on something that's not true, not living — besides, what we call life here did not seem living to me compared with that world — anyway, this feeling should be founded on our relation between the two worlds and on how things make the relation between them easier or more difficult. This would make a great difference in our appraisal of what brings us nearer to the Divine or what separates us from Him. In people too I saw that what helps them to become supramental or hinders them from it, is very different from what our usual moral notions imagine. I felt how... ridiculous we are.

(End of the February 3 experience)

(*Mother speaks to the children:*) There is a continuation of this, a kind of consequence in my consciousness of the experience of third February, but it seemed a little premature to read it now. It will appear later in the April issue,[1] following this.

One thing — I must insist on this — seems to me at the moment to be the most essential difference between our world and the supramental world — and it is only after having gone there consciously, with the consciousness which normally operates here, that this difference has become apparent to me in all its enormity, so to say — everything here, except what goes on within, very deep within, seemed to me absolutely artificial. None of the values of the ordinary physical life are based on truth. And just as to clothe ourselves we have to obtain some cloth and sew clothes to put on when we want to wear them, so too to feed ourselves we need to take things from outside and put them inside our bodies in order to be nourished. In everything our life is artificial.

A true, sincere, spontaneous life like the one in the supramental world, is a springing forth of things from the action of the conscious will, a power over substance which makes it harmonise with what we decide should be. And one who has the power and the knowledge can obtain what he wants, whereas one who does not have them has no artificial means of getting what he desires.

In ordinary life, *everything* is artificial. According to the chance of birth or circumstance, you have a higher or lower position or a more or less comfortable life, not because it is the spontaneous, natural, sincere expression

---

1. *Bulletin*, April 1958. The text is given in an appendix to this talk.

of your way of being and your inner need, but because chance circumstances in life have brought you in contact with these things. An absolutely worthless man may be in a very high position and a man with a marvellous ability to create and organisemay find himself toiling in an absolutely limited and inferior situation, whereas he would be a completely useful person if the world were sincere.

This artificiality, this insincerity, this complete lack of truth became so shockingly apparent to me that... one wonders how, in so false a world, we can have any true evaluations.

But instead of making you sad, morose, rebellious, dissatisfied, there is rather the feeling of what I was saying at the end, of something so laughably ridiculous that for several days I was seized with uncontrollable laughter when I saw things and people! — an uncontrollable laughter, absolutely inexplicable except to myself, at the ridiculousness of things.

When I invited you to a journey into the unknown, a journey of adventure, I did not know I was so close to the truth, and I can promise those who are ready to attempt the adventure that they will make very interesting discoveries.

Appendix

A few days after the experience of February 3, Mother had other experiences which were a kind of continuation of the first one:

Each person carries with himself in his atmosphere what Sri Aurobindo calls the "Censors"; they are in a way permanent delegates of the adverse forces. Their role is to criticise mercilessly every act, every thought, the slightest movement of the consciousness, and to bring you face to face with the most hidden springs of your actions, to bring to light the slightest vibration of a lower kind accompanying what seem to be your purest and highest thoughts and acts.

This is not a question of morality. These gentlemen are not moralising agents although they know very well how to make use of morality! And when they are dealing with a scrupulous conscience, they can harass it without mercy, whispering to it at every minute, "You should not have done this, you should not have done that, you should have done this thing instead, said that thing; now you have spoilt everything, committed an irreparable mistake; see how everything is irretrievably lost now through your fault." They may even take possession of some people's consciousness: you chase away the thought, and there! it comes back two minutes later; you chase it away again and it is still there, all the time

On "Man and the Evolution"

hammering away at you.

Every time I meet these gentlemen I welcome them, for they compel you to be absolutely sincere, they track down the most subtle hypocrisy and make you at every moment face your most secret vibrations. And they are intelligent! — their intelligence infinitely surpasses ours: they know everything, they know how to turn against you the least thought, the least argument, the least action, with a truly wonderful subtlety. Nothing escapes them. But what gives a hostile tinge to these beings is the fact that they are first and foremost defeatists. They always paint the picture for you in the darkest colours; if need be they distort your own intentions. They are truly instruments of sincerity. But they always forget one thing, deliberately, something that they cast far behind as if it did not exist: the divine Grace. They forget prayer, that spontaneous prayer which suddenly springs up from the depths of the being like an intense call, and brings down the Grace and changes the course of things.

And each time you have made some progress, have passed on to a higher level, they make you face once again all the acts of your past life, and in a few months, a few days or a few minutes, they make you go through all your exams once again at a higher level. And it is not enough to brush the thought aside and say, "Oh! I know", and throw a little cloak over it so as not to see. You must face it and conquer, keep your consciousness full of light, without the least tremor, without a word, without the slightest vibration in the cells of the body — and then the attack melts away.

But our ideas of good and evil are so ridiculous! So ridiculous is our notion of what is close to the Divine or far from the Divine! The experience I had the other day, on the third of February, was for me revelatory, I came out of it completely changed. I suddenly understood very many things from the past, actions, parts of my life which had remained inexplicable — in truth, the shortest way from one point to another is not the straight line that men imagine it is!

And all the time the experience lasted, one hour — one hour of that time is long — I was in a state of extraordinary joyfulness, almost in an intoxicated state.... The difference between the two states of consciousness is so great that when you are in one, the other seems unreal, like a dream. When I came back what struck me first of all was the futility of life here; our little conceptions down here seem so laughable, so comical.... We say that some people are mad, but their madness is perhaps a great wisdom, from the supramental point of view, and their behaviour is perhaps nearer to the truth of things — I am not speaking of the obscure madmen whose brains have been damaged, but of many other incomprehensible mad men, the luminous mad: they have wanted to cross the border too quickly and the rest has not followed.

When one looks at the world of men from the supramental consciousness, the predominant feature is a feeling of strangeness, of artificiality — of a world that is absurd because it is artificial. This world is false because its material appearance does not at all express the deeper truth of things. There is a kind of disconnection between the appearance and what is within. In this way, a man with a divine power in the depths of his being may find himself in the position of a slave on the external plane. It is absurd! In the supramental world, on the other hand, it is the will which acts directly on the substance and the substance is obedient to this will. You want to cover yourself: the substance you live in immediately takes the form of a garment to cover you. You want to go from one place to another: your will is enough to transport you without needing any conveyance, any artificial device. Thus, the boat in my experience had no need of any mechanism to move it; it was the will which modified the substance according to its needs. When it was time to land, the wharf took shape of itself. When I wanted to send the groups ashore, those who were to land knew it automatically without my having to say a word, and they came up in turn. Everything went on in silence, there was no need to speak to make oneself understood; but the silence itself on board the ship did not give that impression of artificiality it does here. Here, when one wants silence, one must stop talking; silence is the opposite of sound. There the silence was vibrant, living, active and comprehensive, comprehensible.

The absurd thing here is all the artificial means one must use. Any idiot at all has more power if he has more means to acquire the necessary artifices; whereas in the supramental world, the more conscious one is and the more in touch with the truth of things, the more authority does the will have over substance. The authority is a true authority. If you want a garment you must have the power to make it, a real power. If you do not have this power, well, you remain naked. No device is there to make up for the lack of power. Here, not once in a million times is authority an expression of something true. Everything is formidably stupid.

When I came down again — "came down", it's a way of speaking, for it is neither above nor below, neither inside nor outside; it is... somewhere — it took me some time to readjust myself. I even remember saying to someone, "Now we are going to fall back into our usual stupidity." But I have understood many things and come back from there with a definitive force. Now I know that our way of evaluating things down here, our petty morality, has no relation with the values of the supramental world.

These surface things have nothing dramatic about them. They seem to me more and more like soap-bubbles, especially since the third of February.

There are people who come to me in despair, in tears, in what they call terrible psychological suffering; when I see them like this, I slightly shift the needle in my consciousness which contains you all, and when they go away they are completely comforted. It is just like a compass needle; one shifts the needle a little in the consciousness and it is all over. Of course, it comes back later, out of habit. They are nothing but soap-bubbles.

On "Man and the Evolution"

I have known suffering also, but there was always a part of myself which knew how to stand behind, apart.

The only thing in the world which still seems intolerable to me now, is all the physical deterioration, the physical suffering, the ugliness, the inability to express that capacity for beauty which is in every being. But that too will be conquered one day. There too the power will come one day to shift the needle a little. Only, we must rise higher in consciousness: the deeper one wants to go down into matter, the higher is it necessary to rise in consciousness. That will take time. Sri Aurobindo was surely right when he spoke of a few centuries.

26 February 1958

> *Sweet Mother, you have often spoken about the powers of the sun but you have never said anything about the moon or the stars.*

From what point of view? Symbolically?

> *Yes, Mother.*

That depends on the schools of thought, the periods, the countries.... In a general way, the moon is associated with spiritual force, spiritual progress, spiritual aspiration.

The waxing moon used to be considered as the symbol of spiritual aspiration for transformation, and spiritual plenitude was symbolised by the full moon. Moonlight has always been considered to be very favourable to visions, to poetic inspiration and all other-worldly activity. There are all kinds of stories and legends about the stars — stars which appeared on the day a divine being was born.... But all that is a rather literary kind of symbolism.

There is a fairly widespread belief that stars have a special influence on the destiny of men, to the extent that an entire system of knowledge is founded on this and, according to the different positions of the stars in the sky, it makes quite complete predictions about what will happen in your lifetime.

At an elementary stage of thought, this is expressed by saying that the stars have an influence on our lives. It seems more logical and true to think that it is a sort of notation or recording of the destiny of an individual, for, in the universal unity, everything is interrelated and, if you know how to read the relations between the individual and the universal, you may find in the universal positions of the stars a kind of diagram representing symbolically the life of one individual or another.

Experience proves that this notation which is called in astrology a horoscope is not something absolute and that this destiny is not inevitable, for by taking up yoga and developing spiritually, one escapes from the absolute law of these horoscopes. This would be a kind of notation on the material plane of the relations between universal and individual life, and these relations can be altered by the introduction of a higher plane of consciousness into the material plane of consciousness.

All this is what might be called a half-knowledge, which is a kind of very primitive attempt to grasp the links of interdependence between universal and individual existence. And all these things are much more like languages which enable us to fix a certain half-elaborated knowledge rather than absolute rules or the notation of indisputable facts. They are attempts, endeavours to understand things as they are, but very incomplete attempts — which have a certain attraction for some minds but which are after all only very rough approximations to the truth of things.

If we go deep enough into mental human knowledge,

we realise that all this knowledge as we have it externally in the mental consciousness is scarcely anything more than a language — a fairly complicated one — making it possible for us to understand each other but corresponding only very remotely to the truth of things.

There is a direct approach by identity which is much more effective and, so to say, gives you the concrete key to the whole machinery of things, a direct key that needs no complicated science to express itself — something that corresponds to movements of consciousness and will, which would not need all the mental complications to express themselves. Then the universal reality in its totality becomes a symbol and can be directly perceived in its essence.

5 March 1958

Mother, won't you please speak to us about the "reversal" you have already mentioned to us several times? You said that a reversal was necessary to obtain the new consciousness.

A reversal?

What kind of reversal do we need, now? You said "a reversal of consciousness".

That is a way of speaking. It doesn't mean that you should walk on your head!... It is an image.

Yes, Sri Aurobindo has said this too,[1] so...

---

1. "The necessary condition for the change from the normal animal to the human character of existence would be a development of the physical organisation which would capacitate a rapid progression, a reversal or turnover of the consciousness, a reaching to a new height and a looking down from it at the lower stages, a heightening and widening of capacity which would enable the being to take up the old animal faculties with a larger and more plastic, a human intelligence, and at the same time or later to develop greater and subtler powers proper to the new type of being, powers of reason, reflection, complex observation, organised invention, thought and discovery.... Such a reversal has been made in each radical transition of Nature: Life-Force emerging turns upon Matter, imposes a vital content on the operations of material Energy while it develops also its own new movements

So, if the image leads you to some kind of perception, it is good, but it is not with this (*Mother points to the head*) that you can understand. If it gives you an impression which explains things to you or makes you understand them better, it is all right, but it is not with many words and by going through the brain that you will understand them better.

It is this kind of sensation one has of seeing things in an altogether different way — then one speaks of reversal. It is like... it is always compared with a prism: if you look at it from one side, the light is white, and if you turn it over, it splits up into all its elements. This is something similar.

Words are not good and useful unless through a special grace they put you into contact with the Thing, but in themselves they have no value.

In fact, the ideal condition — which has already been partially realised by some people — is to transmit the essential idea and even something that is higher than the idea: the state — the state of consciousness, of knowledge, of perception — directly through the vibration. When you think, the mental substance vibrates in

---

and operations; Life-Mind emerges in Life-Force and Matter and imposes its content of consciousness on their operations while it develops also its own action and faculties; a new greater emergence and reversal, the emergence of humanity, is in line with Nature's precedents; it would be a new application of the general principle."

The Life Divine, SABCL, Vol. 19, pp. 838-39

a certain way in accordance with the form your consciousness gives to your thought, and it is this vibration which should be perceived by the other mind if it is well attuned.

Indeed, words serve only to draw the attention of the other consciousness or the other centre of consciousness, so that it may be attentive to the vibration and receive it; but if it is not attentive and doesn't have the capacity to receive in comparative silence, you may pour out miles of words without making yourself understood in the least. And there comes a time when the brain, which is very active in emanating certain vibrations, can only receive vibrations which are clear and precise, otherwise it is a kind of vague mixture of something confused, imprecise, which gives the impression of a cloudy, woolly mass and doesn't evoke any idea. So one speaks, the sound is clearly heard, but it conveys nothing — it is not a question of sound, it is a matter of precision in the vibrations.

If you can emanate your thought in a very precise way, if it is something living and *conscious* emanating from your consciousness and going to meet the other consciousness, if, so to speak, you know what you want to say, then it arrives with the same precision, it awakens the corresponding vibration and with the corresponding vibration comes the corresponding thought or idea or state of consciousness, and you understand each other; but if what is emanated is woolly, imprecise, if you do not know very well what you want to say, if you yourself are trying to understand what you want to say, and if, on the other hand, the attention of the hearer is not alert enough or he is busy and active somewhere else, well then, you may talk to each other for hours, you will not understand each other at all!

And in fact this is what happens most often. When you are able to see in the consciousness of others the result of what you have tried to communicate, it always gives you the feeling of... you know what distorting mirrors are? Have you never seen distorting mirrors? Mirrors which make you look taller or fatter, which enlarge one part and reduce another, you are faced with a grotesque caricature of yourself — well, this is exactly what happens: in the other person's consciousness you have an altogether grotesque caricature of what you have said. And people imagine that they have understood each other because they have heard the sound of words, but they haven't communicated.

So, if you want to exercise the least effect on the mental substance, the first thing is to learn how to think clearly, and not a verbal thought which depends on words but a thought which can dispense with words, which can be understood in itself without words, which corresponds to a fact, the fact of a state of consciousness or a fact of knowledge. Just try to think without words, you will see where you stand.

Have you never tried it? Well then, try.

You have an absolutely clear and precise understanding of what you want to communicate to others — it vibrates in a special way, it has the power to give

On "Man and the Evolution" 103

a form to the mental substance; and then, *afterwards*, as a concession to human habits you organise a certain number of words around it to try — there, much lower down — to give a verbal form to the vibration of consciousness. But the verbal form is entirely secondary. It is a kind of covering, a rather crude one, for the power of thought.

What provides the words?

Ah, no! Think clearly, I don't understand you. It is coming like that, like whirls of cotton-wool, and it makes no sense to me.

I see, the word comes out before the thought is formed.

Exactly!

The illustration of this power of thinking is what used to be called the gift of tongues. And in fact this phenomenon did take place and can still do so. You think — that is to say, what I call thinking — quite independently of words, with the clear vision of things and the power to communicate this vision, this phenomenon of consciousness which can be transmitted; now, you are with a large number of people or with a few people, who speak different languages and are used to thinking only in one particular language, for they have been brought up like that; but you project the vibration of your vision, of your understanding, of your experience of things. To attract the attention of the audience you pronounce some words — any language at all, the one most familiar to you, that's of no importance — but your vision and your emanation are precise enough to be transmitted directly to the brain of the others, and in their brain to be automatically translated into their own language. So, outwardly, you are speaking in French or in English, but each one understands in his own language. People think this is a legend — it is not a legend. And it is quite understandable, it is something almost elementary when one goes into the region which I call the region of thought. I am not speaking of supramental things, mind you; it is not a supramental power, it is simply the true realm of thought. That is, you begin to think.

And if you had an audience which also thinks, the phenomenon would take place automatically; only there are very few people who really think. But when they do it powerfully enough, it breaks down the obstacle in the altogether superficial and down-to-earth perception, it rises up like this (*gesture showing a curve*), it goes up into a higher region of perception, and then, in each one, it falls back into the domain of his own language. And each one says with all the sincerity of his experience, "Oh! This person is speaking this language", and another says, "Excuse me, he is speaking that one!" and the third one says, "No, no! He is speaking that other one...." And in fact each one is telling the truth; he probably does not speak any of them except the one he normally uses, or one or two others.... But, it's that, it does this (*same gesture*) and then falls back... like radio-waves.

There, we are going to try. I am going to tell you something, we shall see if you understand.

(*Meditation*)

12 March 1958

> "On the side of consciousness the new manifestation, the human, could be accounted for by an upsurge of concealed Consciousness from the involution in universal Nature. But in that case it must have had some material form already existent for its vehicle of emergence, the vehicle being adapted by the force of the emergence itself to the needs of a new inner creation; or else a rapid divergence from previous physical types or patterns may have brought a new being into existence. But whichever the hypothesis accepted, this means an evolutionary process, — there is only a difference in the method and machinery of the divergence or transition. Or there may have been, on the contrary, not an upsurgence but a descent of mentality from a Mind-plane above us, perhaps the descent of a soul or mental being into terrestrial Nature. The difficulty would then be the appearance of the human body, too complex and difficult an organ to have been suddenly created or manifested; for such a miraculous speed of process, though quite possible on a supraphysical plane of being, does not seem to figure among the normal possibles or potentials of the material Energy. It could only happen there by an intervention of a supraphysical force or law of Nature or by a creator Mind acting with full power and directly on Matter. An action of a supraphysical Force and a

creator may be conceded in every new appearance in Matter; each such appearance is at bottom a miracle operated by a secret Consciousness supported by a veiled Mind-Energy or Life-Energy: but the action is nowhere seen to be direct, overt, self-sufficient; it is always superimposed on an already realised physical basis and acts by an extension of some established process of Nature. It is more conceivable that there was an opening of some existing body to a supraphysical influx so that it was transformed into a new body; but no such event can lightly be assumed to have taken place in the past history of material Nature: in order to happen it would seem to need either the conscious intervention of an invisible mental being to form the body he intended to inhabit or else a previous development of a mental being in Matter itself who would be already able to receive a supraphysical power and impose it on the rigid and narrow formulas of his physical existence. Otherwise we must suppose that there was a pre-existent body already so much evolved as to be fitted for the reception of a vast mental influx or capable of a pliable response to the descent into it of a mental being. But this would suppose a previous evolution of mind in body to the point at which such a receptivity would be possible. It is quite conceivable that such an evolution from below and such a descent from above cooperated in the appearance of humanity in earth-nature. The secret psychical entity already there in the animal might have itself

> *called down the mental being, the Mind-Purusha, into the realm of living Matter in order to take up the vital mental energy already at work and lift it into a higher mentality. But this would still be a process of evolution, the higher plane only intervening to assist the appearance and enlargement of its own principle in terrestrial Nature."*
>
> The Life Divine, SABCL, Vol. 19, pp. 839-40

The difficulty of the problem is that only a mental being could take an interest in this process of transformation and creation, and that the mental consciousness in the animal species was not sufficient for it to take an interest in this process.

Animals had no means of noting what was happening, of taking it into consideration and remembering it. And that is why this part of the earth's history has almost disappeared. A mental capacity like man's must intervene to make it possible to follow the course of this transformation and retain a memory of it.... In fact, more is imagined than remembered. It is quite obvious that the psychic being has gone through all that, but it has not kept a mental memory of it. The memory of the psychic being is a psychic memory which is of an altogether different kind; it is not historical like mental memory which can keep a precise record of what takes place.

But now that we are on the threshold of the new transformation, the new emergence as it is called here, and now that we are going to witness the process of transformation between the human mental being and the supramental being, we shall profit by this historical ability of the mind which will follow what happens and take note of it. So, from that point of view also, the phenomenon which is taking place now is absolutely unique in the history of the earth, and probably — almost certainly — when we have followed the process of this transformation to the very end, we shall have the key to all the former transformations; that is, everything that we are trying to understand at present, we shall know for certain when the process is repeated, this time between the mental and the supramental being.

You are therefore invited to a very special development of the capacity for observation, so that all this may not take place in a half-dream and you awaken to a new life without even knowing how things have happened.

One must be very vigilant, wide awake, and instead of being interested in little inner psychological phenomena which are... quite antiquated — they belong to an entire period of human history which anyway has lost all its novelty — it would be better to be more attentive to things of greater general import, things more subtle, more impersonal which would put you in the midst of new discoveries of a very special interest.

Open the eyes of the subtle intelligence, and without prejudice or preference, without egoism and without attachment, look at what is happening day by day.

19 March 1958

"Next, it may be conceded that each type or pattern of consciousness and being in the body, once established, has to be faithful to the law of being of that type, to its own design and rule of nature. But it may also very well be that part of the law of the human type is its impulse towards self-exceeding, that the means for a conscious transition has been provided for among the spiritual powers of man; the possession of such a capacity may be a part of the plan on which the creative Energy has built him. It may be conceded that what man has up till now principally done is to act within the circle of his nature, on a spiral of nature-movement, sometimes descending, sometimes ascending, — there has been no straight line of progress, no indisputable, fundamental or radical exceeding of his past nature: what he has done is to sharpen, subtilise, make a more and more complex and plastic use of his capacities. It cannot truly be said that there has been no such thing as human progress since man's appearance or even in his recent ascertainable history; for however great the ancients, however supreme some of their achievements and creations, however impressive their powers of spirituality, of intellect or of character, there has been in later developments an increasing subtlety, complexity, manifold development of knowledge and possibility in man's achievements, in his

politics, society, life, science, metaphysics, knowledge of all kinds, art, literature; even in his spiritual endeavour, less surprisingly lofty and less massive in power of spirituality than that of the ancients, there has been this increasing subtlety, plasticity, sounding of depths, extension of seeking. There have been falls from a high type of culture, a sharp temporary descent into a certain obscurantism, cessations of the spiritual urge, plunges into a barbaric natural materialism; but these are temporary phenomena, at worst a downward curve of the spiral of progress. This progress has not indeed carried the race beyond itself, into a self-exceeding, a transformation of the mental being. But that was not to be expected; for the action of evolutionary Nature in a type of being and consciousness is first to develop the type to its utmost capacity by just such a subtilisation and increasing complexity till it is ready for her bursting of the shell, the ripened decisive emergence, reversal, turning over of consciousness on itself that constitutes a new stage in the evolution. If it be supposed that her next step is the spiritual and supramental being, the stress of spirituality in the race may be taken as a sign that that is Nature's intention, the sign too of the capacity of man to operate in himself or aid her to operate the transition. If the appearance in animal being of a type similar in some respects to the ape kind but already from the beginning endowed with the elements of humanity was the method of the human evolution, the appearance

> *in the human being of a spiritual type resembling mental-animal humanity but already with the stamp of the spiritual aspiration on it would be the obvious method of Nature for the evolutionary production of the spiritual and supramental being."*
> The Life Divine, SABCL, Vol. 19, pp. 841-42

One thing seems obvious, humanity has reached a certain state of general tension — tension in effort, in action, even in daily life — with such an excessive hyperactivity, so widespread a trepidation, that mankind as a whole seems to have come to a point where it must either break through the resistance and emerge into a new consciousness or else fall back into an abyss of darkness and inertia.

This tension is so complete and so widespread that something obviously has to break. It cannot go on in this way. We may take it as a sure sign of the infusion into matter of a new principle of force, consciousness, power, which by its very pressure is producing this acute state. Outwardly, we could expect the old methods used by Nature when she wants to bring about an upheaval; but there is a new characteristic, which of course is only visible in an *élite*, but even this *élite* is fairly widespread — it is not localised at one point, at one place in the world; we find traces of it in all countries, all over the world: the will to find a new, higher, progressive solution, an effort to rise towards a vaster, more comprehensive perfection.

Certain ideas of a more general nature, of a wider,

perhaps more "collective" kind, are being worked out and are acting in the world. And both things go together: a possibility of a greater and more total destruction, a reckless inventiveness which increases the possibility of catastrophe, a castastrophe which would be on a far greater scale than it has ever been; and, at the same time, the birth or rather the manifestation of much higher and more comprehensive ideas and acts of will which, when they are heard, will bring a wider, vaster, more complete, more perfect remedy than before.

This struggle, this conflict between the constructive forces of the ascending evolution of a more and more perfect and divine realisation, and the more and more destructive, powerfully destructive forces — forces that are mad beyond all control — is more and more obvious, marked, visible, and it is a kind of race or struggle as to which will reach the goal first. It would seem that all the adverse, anti-divine forces, the forces of the vital world, have descended on the earth, are making use of it as their field of action, and that at the same time a new, higher, more powerful spiritual force has also descended on earth to bring it a new life. This makes the struggle more acute, more violent, more visible, but it seems also more definitive, and that is why we can hope to reach an early solution.

There was a time, not so long ago, when the spiritual aspiration of man was turned towards a silent, inactive peace, detached from all worldly things, a flight from life, precisely to avoid battle, to rise above the struggle, escape all effort; it was a spiritual peace in which, along with the cessation of all tension, struggle, effort, there ceased also suffering in all its forms, and this was considered to be the true and only expression of a spiritual and divine life. It was considered to be the divine grace, the divine help, the divine intervention. And even now, in this age of anguish, tension, hypertension, this sovereign peace is the best received aid of all, the most welcome, the solace people ask and hope for. For many it is still the true sign of a divine intervention, of divine grace.

In fact, no matter what one wants to realise, one must begin by establishing this perfect and immutable peace; it is the basis from which one must work; but unless one is dreaming of an exclusive, personal and egoistic liberation, one cannot stop there. There is another aspect of the divine grace, the aspect of progress which will be victorious over all obstacles, the aspect which will propel humanity to a new realisation, which will open the doors of a new world and make it possible not only for a chosen few to benefit by the divine realisation but for their influence, their example, their power to bring to the rest of mankind new and better conditions.

This opens up roads of realisation into the future, possibilities which are already foreseen, when an entire part of humanity, the one which has opened consciously or unconsciously to the new forces, is lifted up, as it were, into a higher, more harmonious, more perfect life.... Even if individual transformation is not always permissible or possible, there will be a kind of general uplifting, a harmonisation of the whole, which will make it possible for a new order, a new harmony to be established and for the anguish of the present disorder and struggle to disappear and be replaced by an order which will allow a harmonious functioning of the whole.

There will be other consequences which will tend to eliminate in an opposite way what the intervention of the mind in life has created, the perversions, the ugliness, the whole mass of distortions which have increased suffering, misery, moral poverty, an entire area of sordid and repulsive misery which makes a whole part of human life into something so frightful. That must disappear. This is what makes humanity in so many ways infinitely worse than animal life in its simplicity and the natural spontaneity and harmony that it has in spite of everything. Suffering in animals is never so miserable and sordid as it is in an entire section of humanity which has been perverted by the use of a mentality exclusively at the service of egoistic needs.

We must rise above, spring up into Light and Harmony or fall back, down into the simplicity of a healthy unperverted animal life.

When this talk was first published in 1958, Mother added the following note on the "uplifting" of an entire part of humanity by the action of the new forces:

But those who cannot be lifted up, those who refuse to progress, will automatically lose the use of the mental consciousness and will fall back to a sub-human level.

I shall tell you about an experience I had which will help you to understand better. It was shortly after the supramental experience of the third of February,[1] and I was still in the state in which things of the physical world seemed so far off, so absurd. A group of visitors had asked permission to come to me and one evening they came to the Playground. They were rich people, that is, they had more money than they needed to live on. Among them there was a woman in a sari; she was very fat, her sari was arranged so as to hide her body. As she was bending down to receive my blessings, one corner of the sari came open, uncovering a part of her body, a naked belly — an enormous one. I felt a real shock.... There are corpulent people who have nothing repugnant about them, but I suddenly saw the perversion, the rottenness that this belly concealed, it was like a huge abscess, expressing greed, vice, depraved taste, sordid desire, which finds its satisfaction as no animal would, in grossness and especially in perversity. I saw the perversion of a depraved mind at the service of the lowest appetites. Then, all of a sudden, something sprang up from me, a prayer, like a Veda: "O Lord, this is what must disappear!"

One understands very well that physical misery, the unequal distribution of the goods of this world could be changed, one can imagine economic and social solutions which could remedy this, but it is that misery,

---

1. See Appendix to the talk of February 19.

the mental misery, the vital perversion, it is that which cannot change, doesn't want to change. And those who belong to this type of humanity are condemned in advance to disintegration.

That is the meaning of original sin: the perversion which began with the mind.

That part of humanity, of human consciousness, which is capable of uniting with the supermind and liberating itself, will be completely transformed — it is advancing towards a future reality which is not yet expressed in its outer form; the part which is closest to Nature, to animal simplicity, will be reabsorbed into Nature and thoroughly assimilated. But the corrupted part of human consciousness which allows perversion through its misuse of the mind will be abolished.

This type of humanity is part of an unfruitful attempt — which must be eliminated — just as there have been other abortive species which have disappeared in the course of universal history.

Certain prophets in the past have had this apocalyptic vision but, as usual, things were mixed, and they did not have together with their vision of the apocalypse the vision of the supramental world which will come to raise up the part of humanity which consents and to transform this physical world. So, to give hope to those who have been born into it, into this perverted part of human consciousness, they have taught redemption through faith: those who have faith in the sacrifice of the Divine in Matter will be automatically saved, in another world — by faith alone, without understanding, without intelligence. They have not seen the supramental world nor that the great Sacrifice of the Divine in Matter is the sacrifice of involution which must culminate in the total revelation of the Divine in Matter itself.

26 March 1958

"It is pertinently suggested that if such an evolutionary culmination is intended and man is to be its medium, it will only be a few especially evolved human beings who will form the new type and move towards the new life; that once done, the rest of humanity will sink back from a spiritual aspiration no longer necessary for Nature's purpose and remain quiescent in its normal status. It can equally be reasoned that the human gradation must be preserved if there is really an ascent of the soul by reincarnation through the evolutionary degrees towards the spiritual summit; for otherwise the most necessary of all the intermediate steps will be lacking. It must be conceded at once that there is not the least probability or possibility of the whole human race rising in a block to the supramental level; what is suggested is nothing so revolutionary and astonishing, but only the capacity in the human mentality, when it has reached a certain level or a certain point of stress of the evolutionary impetus, to press towards a higher plane of consciousness and its embodiment in the being. The being will necessarily undergo by this embodiment a change from the normal constitution of its nature, a change certainly of its mental and emotional and sensational constitution and also to a great extent of the body-consciousness and the physical conditioning of our life and energies; but the change of consciousness will be the chief factor,

> *the initial movement, the physical modification will be a subordinate factor, a consequence. This transmutation of the consciousness will always remain possible to the human being when the flame of the soul, the psychic kindling, becomes potent in heart and mind and the nature is ready. The spiritual aspiration is innate in man; for he is, unlike the animal, aware of imperfection and limitation and feels that there is something to be attained beyond what he now is: this urge towards self-exceeding is not likely ever to die out totally in the race. The human mental status will be always there, but it will be there not only as a degree in the scale of rebirth, but as an open step towards the spiritual and supramental status."*
>
> *The Life Divine*, SABCL, Vol. 19, pp. 842-43

It is obvious that what especially characterises man is this mental capacity of watching himself live. The animal lives spontaneously, automatically, and if it watches itself live, it must be to a very minute and insignificant degree, and that is why it is peaceful and does not worry. Even if an animal is suffering because of an accident or an illness, this suffering is reduced to a minimum by the fact that it does not observe it, does not project it in its consciousness and into the future, does not imagine things about its illness or its accident.

With man there has begun this perpetual worrying about what is going to happen, and this worry is the principal, if not the sole cause of his torment. With this objectivising consciousness there has begun anxiety, painful imaginations, worry, torment, anticipation of future catastrophes, with the result that most men — and not the least conscious, the most conscious — live in perpetual torment. Man is too conscious to be indifferent, he is not conscious enough to know what will happen. Truly it could be said without fear of making a mistake that of all earth's creatures he is the most miserable. The human being is used to being like that because it is an atavistic state which he has inherited from his ancestors, but it is truly a miserable condition. And it is only with this spiritual capacity of rising to a higher level and replacing the animal's unconsciousness by a spiritual super-consciousness that there comes into the being not only the capacity to see the goal of existence and to foresee the culmination of the effort but also a clear-sighted trust in a higher spiritual power to which one can surrender one's whole being, entrust oneself, give the responsibility for one's life and future and so abandon all worries.

Of course, it is impossible for man to fall back to the level of the animal and lose the consciousness he has acquired; therefore, for him there is only one means, one way to get out of this condition he is in, which I call a miserable one, and to emerge into a higher state where worry is replaced by a trusting surrender and the certitude of a luminous culmination — this way is to change the consciousness.

Truly speaking there is no condition more miserable than being responsible for an existence to which one doesn't have the key, that is, of which one doesn't have the threads that can guide and solve the problems. The animal sets itself no problems: it just lives. Its instinct drives it, it relies on a collective consciousness which has an innate knowledge and is higher than itself, but it is automatic, spontaneous, it has no need to will something and make an effort to bring it about, it is quite naturally like that, and as it is not responsible for its life, it does not worry. With man is born the sense of having to depend on himself, and as he does not have the necessary knowledge the result is a perpetual torment. This torment can come to an end only with a total surrender to a higher consciousness than his own to which he can totally entrust himself, hand over his worries and leave the care of guiding his life and organising everything.

How can a problem be solved when one doesn't have the necessary knowledge? And the unfortunate thing is that man believes that he has to resolve all the problems of his life, and he does not have the knowledge needed to do it. That is the source, the origin of all his troubles — that perpetual question, "What should I do?..." which is followed by another one still more acute, "What is going to happen?" and at the same time, more or less, the inability to answer.

That is why all spiritual disciplines begin with the necessity of surrendering all responsibility and relying on a higher principle. Otherwise peace is impossible.

And yet, consciousness has been given to man so that he can progress, can discover what he doesn't know, develop into what he has not yet become; and

On "Man and the Evolution"

so it may be said that there is a higher state than that of an immobile and static peace: it is a trust total enough for one to keep the will to progress, to preserve the effort for progress while ridding it of all anxiety, all care for results and consequences. This is one step ahead of the methods which may be called "quietist", which are founded on the rejection of all activity and a plunging into an immobility and inner silence, which forsake all life because it has been suddenly felt that without peace one can't have any inner realisation and, quite naturally, one thought that one couldn't have peace so long as one was living in outer conditions, in the state of anxiety in which problems are set and cannot be solved, for one does not have the knowledge to do so. The next step is to face the problem, but with the calm and certitude of an absolute trust in the supreme Power which knows, and can make you act. And then, instead of abandoning action, one can act in a higher peace that is strong and dynamic. This is what could be called a new aspect of the divine intervention in life, a new form of intervention of the divine forces in existence, a new aspect of spiritual realisation.

2 April 1958

Mother, you said that when one consciously makes a mistake it is much more serious than if one makes it unconsciously.

When you make a mistake because you don't know that it is a mistake, through ignorance, it is obvious that when you learn that it is a mistake, when the ignorance has gone and you have goodwill, you don't make the mistake any more, and so you come out of the condition in which you could make it. But if you know it is a mistake and make it, this means that there is something perverse in you which has deliberately chosen to be on the side of confusion or bad will or even the anti-divine forces.

And it is quite obvious that if one chooses to be on the side of the anti-divine forces or is so weak and inconsistent that one can't resist the temptation to be on their side, it is infinitely more serious from the psychological point of view. This means that somewhere something has been corrupted: either an adverse force is already established in you or else you have an innate sympathy for these forces. And it is much more difficult to correct that than to correct an ignorance.

Correcting an ignorance is like eliminating darkness: you light a lamp, the darkness disappears. But to make a mistake once again when you know it is a mistake, is as if someone lighted a lamp and you deliberately put it out.... That corresponds exactly to bringing the darkness back deliberately. For the argument of weakness does not hold. The divine Grace is always there to help those who have decided to correct themselves, and they cannot say, "I am too weak to correct myself." They can say that they still haven't taken the resolution to correct themselves, that somewhere in the being there is something that has *not decided* to do it, and that is what is serious.

The argument of weakness is an excuse. The Grace is there to give the supreme strength to whoever takes the resolution.

That means an insincerity, it does not mean a weakness. And insincerity is always an open door for the adversary. That means there is some secret sympathy with what is perverse. And that is what is serious.

In the case of ignorance which is to be enlightened, it is enough, as I said, to light the lamp. In the case of conscious relapse, what is necessary is a cauterisation.

9 April 1958

> *Sweet Mother, with the human mind is it possible to recognise another person's soul?*

Things are not so clear-cut and separate as they are in speaking; that is just why it is quite difficult to see very distinctly and clearly in oneself the different parts of the being, unless one has had a very long training and a long discipline of study and observation. There are no watertight compartments between the soul and the mind, the vital and even the physical. There is an infiltration of the soul into the mind. In some people it is even quite considerable, it is perceptible. So, the part of the mind which has a kind of sensibility, of subtle contact with the psychic being, is capable of feeling the presence of the soul in others.

Those who have the ability to enter to a certain extent into the consciousness of others to the point of being able to see or feel directly their thought, their mental activity, who can enter the mental atmosphere of others without needing to use words to make themselves understood, can easily differentiate between someone whose soul is active and someone whose soul is asleep. The activity of the soul gives a special colouring to the mental activity — it is lighter, more comprehensive and luminous — so that can be felt. For instance, by looking into someone's eyes you can say with some certainty that this person has a living soul or that you don't see his soul in his eyes. Many people can feel — "many", I mean among evolved people — can say that. But naturally, to know exactly how far somebody's soul is awake and active, how far it rules the being, is the master, one must have the psychic consciousness oneself, for that alone can judge definitively. But it is not altogether impossible to have that sort of inner vibration which makes you say, "Oh! This person has a soul."

Now, obviously, most often what people — unless they are initiated — call "soul" is the vital activity. If someone has a strong, active, obstinate vital which rules the body's activities, which has a very living or intense contact with people and things and events, if he has a marked taste for art, for all expressions of beauty, we are generally tempted to say and believe, "Oh! He has a living soul"; but it is not his soul, it is his vital being which is alive and dominates the activities of the body. That is the first difference between someone who is beginning to be developed and those who are still in the inertia and tamas of the purely material life. This gives, first to the appearance and also to the activity, a kind of vibration, of intensity of vibration, which often creates the impression that this person has a living soul; but it is not that, it is his vital which is developed, which has a special capacity, is stronger than the physical inertia and gives an intensity of vibration and life and action that those whose vital being is not developed do not possess. This confusion between the vital activity and the soul is a very frequent one.... The vital vibration is much more easily perceptible to the human consciousness than the vibration of the soul.

To perceive the soul in someone, as a rule the mind must be very quiet — very quiet, for when it is active, its vibrations are seen, not the vibration of the soul.

And then, when you look at someone who is conscious of his soul, and lives in his soul, if you look like this, the impression you have is of descending, of entering deep, deep, deep into the person, far, far, far, far within; while usually when you look into someone's eyes, you very soon come to a surface which vibrates and answers your look, but you don't have that feeling of going down, down, down, down, going deep as into a hole and very far, very, very, very far within, so you have... a small, very quiet response. Otherwise, usually you enter — there are eyes you cannot enter, they are closed like a door; but still there are eyes which are open — you enter and then, quite close behind, you come to something vibrating there, like this, shining at times, vibrating. And then, that's it; if you make a mistake, you say, "Oh! He has a living soul" — it is not that, it is his vital.

In order to find the soul you must go in this way (*gesture of going deep within*), like this, draw back from the surface, withdraw deep within and enter, enter, enter, go down, down, down into a very deep hole, silent, immobile, and there, there's a kind of... something warm, quiet, rich in substance and very still, and very full, like a sweetness — that is the soul.

And if one is insistent and is conscious oneself, then there comes a kind of plenitude which gives the feeling of something complete that contains unfathomable depths in which, should one enter, one feels that many secrets would be revealed... like the reflection in very peaceful waters of something that is eternal. And one no longer feels limited by time.

One has the feeling of having always been and of being for eternity.

That is when one has touched the core of the soul.

And if the contact has been conscious and complete enough, it liberates you from the bondage of outer form; you no longer feel that you live only because you have a body. That is usually the ordinary sensation of the being, to be so tied to this outer form that when one thinks of "myself" one thinks of the body. That is the usual thing. The personal reality is the body's reality. It is only when one has made an effort for inner development and tried to find something that is a little more stable in one's being, that one can begin to feel that this "something" which is permanently conscious throughout all ages and all change, this something must be "myself". But that already requires a study that is rather deep. Otherwise if you think "I am going to do this", "I need that", it is always your body, a small kind of will which is a mixture of sensations, of more or less confused sentimental reactions, and still more confused thoughts which form a mixture and are animated by an impulse, an attraction, a desire, some sort of a will; and all that momentarily becomes "myself" — but not directly, for one does not conceive this "myself" as independent of the head, the trunk, the arms and legs and all that moves — it is very closely linked.

It is only after having thought much, seen much, studied much, observed much that you begin to realise that the one is more or less independent of the other and that the will behind can make it either act or not act, and you begin not to be completely identified with the movement, the action, the realisation — that something is floating. But you have to observe much to see that.

And then you must observe much more still to see that this, the second thing that is there, this kind of active conscious will, is set in motion by "something else" which watches, judges, decides and tries to found its decisions on knowledge — that happens even much later. And so, when you begin to see this "something else", you begin to see that it has the power to set in motion the second thing, which is an active will; and not only that, but that it has a very direct and very important action on the reactions, the feelings, the sensations, and that finally it can have control over all the movements of the being — this part which watches, observes, judges and decides.

That is the beginning of control.

When one becomes conscious of that, one has seized the thread, and when one speaks of control, one can know, "Ah! Yes, this is what has the power of control."

This is how one learns to look at oneself.

16 April 1958

"In the previous stages of the evolution Nature's first care and effort had to be directed towards a change in the physical organisation, for only so could there be a change of consciousness; this was a necessity imposed by the insufficiency of the force of consciousness already in formation to effect a change in the body. But in man a reversal is possible, indeed inevitable; for it is through his consciousness, through its transmutation and no longer through a new bodily organism as a first instrumentation that the evolution can and must be effected. In the inner reality of things a change of consciousness was always the major fact, the evolution has always had a spiritual significance and the physical change was only instrumental; but this relation was concealed by the first abnormal balance of the two factors, the body of the external Inconscience outweighing and obscuring in importance the spiritual element, the conscious being. But once the balance has been righted, it is no longer the change of body that must precede the change of consciousness; the consciousness itself by its mutation will necessitate and operate whatever mutation is needed for the body. It has to be noted that the human mind has already shown a capacity to aid Nature in the evolution of new types of plant and animal; it has created new forms of its environment, developed by knowledge

and discipline considerable changes in its own mentality. It is not an impossibility that man should aid Nature consciously also in his own spiritual and physical evolution and transformation. The urge to it is already there and partly effective, though still incompletely understood and accepted by the surface mentality; but one day it may understand, go deeper within itself and discover the means, the secret energy, the intended operation of the Consciousness-Force within which is the hidden reality of what we call Nature....

"If a spiritual unfolding on earth is the hidden truth of our birth into Matter, if it is fundamentally an evolution of consciousness that has been taking place in Nature, then man as he is cannot be the last term of that evolution: he is too imperfect an expression of the Spirit, Mind itself a too limited form and instrumentation; Mind is only a middle term of consciousness, the mental being can only be a transitional being. If, then, man is incapable of exceeding mentality, he must be surpassed and Supermind and superman must manifest and take the lead of the creation. But if his mind is capable of opening to what exceeds it, then there is no reason why man himself should not arrive at Supermind and supermanhood or at least lend his mentality, life and body to an evolution of that greater term of the Spirit manifesting in Nature."

The Life Divine, SABCL, Vol. 19, pp. 843-44; 846-47

Anyway, we have now reached a certitude since there is already a beginning of realisation. We have the proof that in certain conditions the ordinary state of humanity can be exceeded and a new state of consciousness worked out which enables at least a conscious relation between mental and supramental man.

It can be asserted with certainty that there will be an intermediate specimen between the mental and the supramental being, a kind of superman who will still have the qualities and in part the nature of man, that is, who will still belong in his most external form to the human being with its animal origin, but will transform his consciousness sufficiently to belong in his realisation and activity to a new race, a race of supermen. This species may be considered a transitional species, for one can foresee that it will discover the means of producing new beings without going through the old animal method, and these beings — who will have a truly spiritual birth — will constitute the elements of the new race, the supramental race.

So we could call supermen those who, in their origin, still belong to the old method of generation but in their achievement are in conscious and active contact with the new world of supramental realisation.

It seems — it is even certain — that the very substance which will constitute this intermediate world that is already being built up, is richer, more powerful, more luminous, more resistant, with certain subtler, more penetrating new qualities, and a kind of innate capacity of universality, as if its degree of subtlety and refinement allowed the perception of vibrations in a much wider, if not altogether total way, and it removes the sensation of division one has with the old substance, the ordinary mental substance. There is a subtlety of vibration which makes global, universal perception a spontaneous and natural thing. The sense of division, of separation, disappears quite naturally and spontaneously with that substance. And that substance is at present almost universally diffused in the earth atmosphere. It is perceptible in the waking state, simply with a little concentration and a kind of absorption of consciousness, if this is retracted, withdrawn from the ordinary externalisation which seems more and more artificial and false. This externalisation, this perception which formerly was natural, now seems false, unreal and completely artificial; it does not at all answer to things as they are, it belongs to a movement which does not correspond to anything really true.

This new perception is asserting itself more and more, becoming more and more natural, and it is even sometimes difficult to recapture the old way of being, as though it were vanishing into a misty past — something which is on the point of ceasing to exist.

One may conclude from this that the moment a body, which was of course formed by the old animal method, is capable of living this consciousness naturally and spontaneously, without effort, without going out of itself, it proves that this is not one single exceptional case but simply the forerunner of a realisation which, even if it is not altogether general, can at least be shared

On "Man and the Evolution"

by a certain number of individuals who, besides, as soon as they share it, will lose the perception of being separate individuals and become a living collectivity.

This new realisation is proceeding with what one might call a lightning speed, for if we consider time in the ordinary way, only two years have passed — a little more than two years — from the time the supramental substance penetrated into the earth atmosphere to the time the change in the quality of the earth atmosphere took place.

If things go on advancing at this speed, it seems more than possible, almost evident, that what Sri Aurobindo wrote in a letter is a prophetic announcement: The supramental consciousness will enter a phase of realising power in 1967.[1]

---

1. "4-5-67 is the year of complete realisation." *Letters on Yoga*, SABCL, Vol. 22, p. 35

23 April 1958

> *Sweet Mother, when we make an effort to do better but don't see any progress, we feel discouraged. What is the best thing to do?*

Not to be discouraged! Despondency leads nowhere.

To begin with, the first thing to tell yourself is that you are almost entirely incapable of knowing whether you are making progress or not, for very often what seems to us to be a state of stagnation is a long — sometimes long, but in any case not endless — preparation for a leap forward. We sometimes seem to be marking time for weeks or months, and then suddenly something that was being prepared makes its appearance, and we see that there is quite a considerable change and on several points at a time.

As with everything in yoga, the effort for progress must be made for the love of the effort for progress. The joy of effort, the aspiration for progress must be enough in themselves, quite independent of the result. Everything one does in yoga must be done for the joy of doing it, and not in view of the result one wants to obtain.... Indeed, in life, always, in all things, the result does not belong to us. And if we want to keep the right attitude, we must act, feel, think, strive spontaneously, for that is what we must do, and not in view of the result to be obtained.

As soon as we think of the result we begin to bargain

On "Man and the Evolution"

and that takes away all sincerity from the effort. You make an effort to progress because you feel within you the need, the *imperative* need to make an effort and progress; and this effort is the gift you offer to the Divine Consciousness in you, the Divine Consciousness in the Universe, it is your way of expressing your gratitude, offering your self; and whether this results in progress or not is of no importance. You will progress when it is decided that the time has come to progress and not because you desire it.

If you wish to progress, if you make an effort to control yourself for instance, to overcome certain defects, weaknesses, imperfections, and if you expect to get a more or less immediate result from your effort, your effort loses all sincerity, it becomes a bargaining. You say, "See! I am going to make an effort, but that's because I want this in exchange for my effort." You are no longer spontaneous, no longer natural.

So there are two things to remember. First, we are incapable of judging what the result ought to be. If we put our trust in the Divine, if we say... if we say, "Well now, I am going to give everything, everything, all I can give, effort, concentration, and He will judge what has to be given in exchange or even whether anything should be given in exchange, and I do not know what the result should be." Before we transform anything in ourselves, are we quite sure of the direction, the way, the form that this transformation should take? — Not at all. So, it is only our imagination and usually we greatly limit the result to be obtained and make it altogether petty, mean, superficial, relative. We do not know what the result can truly be, what it ought to be. We know it later. When it comes, when the change takes place, then if we look back, we say, "Ah! That's it, that is what I was moving towards" — but we know it only later. Before that we only have vague imaginations which are quite superficial and childish in comparison with the true progress, the true transformation.

So we say, first point: we have an aspiration but we don't really know the true result we ought to obtain. Only the Divine can know that.

And secondly, if we tell the Divine, "I am giving you my effort, but, you know, in exchange I must make progress, otherwise I won't give you anything at all!" — that is bargaining. That's all.

(Silence)

A spontaneous act, done because one cannot do otherwise, and done as an offering of goodwill, is the only one which truly has any value.

30 April 1958

As I had foreseen, I have received a shower of questions to oblige me to explain mentally my supramental experience of the third of February.[1]

You want to make me speak and mentalise the experience until a new system is established and you can sit down comfortably in your new mental construction.... I am sorry to have to disappoint you but this is absolutely impossible. And if you want to understand what I have written, well, make an effort to have a supramental consciousness.

That is all I have to say to you.

And beware of the mania of wanting to replace an old dogma by a new one and saying, "Oh! All that was false, but now we are going to work out a fine practical guide to conduct which will be the true one."

Well, a mental construction will never be true, and I refuse to make one. I was obliged to use words which men understand, but I did it in the most incoherent way possible! in order not to be too mental, and I refuse to be coherent in the mental fashion; and that, not only for the questions I have here or those I have received in letters, but for all those that are still to come on the same subject. So it will be useless to ask me any.

I would advise the same thing to everyone: Make an effort, work, open yourself, give yourself up entirely to

1. See pp. 271-276.

the new Force, and a day will come when you will have the experience.

With the experience you will understand precisely how useless the questions were.

ON "THE EVOLUTION OF THE SPIRITUAL MAN"

7 May 1958

"In the earliest stages of evolutionary Nature we are met by the dumb secrecy of her inconscience; there is no revelation of any significance or purpose in her works, no hint of any other principles of being than that first formulation which is her immediate preoccupation and seems to be for ever her only business: for in her primal works Matter alone appears, the sole dumb and stark cosmic reality. A Witness of creation, if there had been one conscious but uninstructed, would only have seen appearing out of a vast abyss of an apparent nonexistence an Energy busy with the creation of Matter, a material world and material objects, organising the infinity of the Inconscient into the scheme of a boundless universe or a system of countless universes that stretched around him into Space without any certain end or limit, a tireless creation of nebulae and star-clusters and suns and planets, existing only for itself, without a sense in it, empty of cause or purpose. It might have seemed to him a stupendous machinery without a use, a mighty meaningless movement, an aeonic spectacle without a witness, a cosmic edifice without an inhabitant; for he would have seen no sign of an indwelling Spirit, no being for whose delight it was made. A creation of this kind could only be the outcome of an inconscient Energy or an illusion-cinema, a shadow-play or puppet-play of forms

> *reflected on a superconscient indifferent Absolute. He would have seen no evidence of a soul and no hint of Mind or Life in this immeasurable and interminable display of Matter. It would not have seemed to him possible or imaginable that there could at all be in this desert universe for ever inanimate and insensible an outbreak of teeming life, a first vibration of something occult and incalculable, alive and conscious, a secret spiritual entity feeling its way towards the surface."*
>
> *The Life Divine*, SABCL, Vol. 19, pp. 848-49

I did not understand this sentence, Sweet Mother: "In the earliest stages of evolutionary Nature we are met by the dumb secrecy of her inconscience." What is this secrecy, Sweet Mother?

The intention of Nature?... It is what Sri Aurobindo has said from the beginning, that, hidden in the depths, at the core of matter, there is the Divine Presence and that the whole terrestrial evolution is made to prepare the return of the creation to its origin, to this Divine Presence which is at the centre of everything — that is the intention of Nature.

The universe is an objectivisation of the Supreme, as if He had objectivised himself outside of himself in order to see himself, to live himself, to know himself, and so that there might be an existence and a consciousness capable of recognising him as their origin and uniting consciously with him to manifest him in the becoming.

On "The Evolution of the Spiritual Man"

There is no other reason for the universe. The earth is a kind of symbolic crystallisation of universal life, a reduction, a concentration, so that the work of evolution may be easier to do and follow. And if we see the history of the earth, we can understand why the universe has been created. It is the Supreme growing aware of himself in an eternal Becoming; and the goal is the union of the created with the Creator, a union that is conscious, willing and free, in the Manifestation.

That is the secret of Nature. Nature is the executive Force, it is she who does the work.

And she takes up this creation, which appears to be totally inconscient but which contains the Supreme Consciousness and sole Reality and she works so that all this can develop, become self-aware and realise itself fully. But she does not show it from the very beginning. It develops gradually, and that is why at the start it is a secret which will be unveiled as it nears the end. And man has reached a point in the evolution high enough for this secret to be unveiled and for what was done in an apparent inconscience to be done consciously, willingly, and therefore much more rapidly and in the joy of realisation.

In man one can already see that the spiritual reality is being developed and that it is going to express itself totally and freely. Formerly, in the animal and the plant, it was... it was necessary to be very clear-sighted to see it, but man is himself conscious of this spiritual reality, at least in the higher part of his human existence. Man is beginning to know what the Supreme Origin wants of him and is collaborating in carrying it out.

Nature wants the creation to become conscious of being the Creator himself in an objectivisation, that is to say, there is no difference between the Creator and the Creation, and the goal is a conscious and realised union. That is the secret of Nature.

> *Mother, here Sri Aurobindo writes: "the dumb secrecy of her inconscience". Why her "inconscience"?*

Whose inconscience?

> *Nature's.*

No, Nature is not unconscious, but she has an appearance of unconsciousness. It began with the inconscience, but in the depths of the inconscience there was consciousness, and this consciousness is gradually developing.[1] For instance, mineral nature, stones, earth, metals, water, air, all this seems to be quite unconscious, although if one observes closely... And now science is discovering that this is only an appearance, that all this is only concentrated energy, and of course it is a conscious force which has produced all this. But apparently, when we see a rock, we don't think it is conscious, it does not give the impression of being conscious, it seems

---

1. When this talk was first published, Mother made the following correction: "It is not the consciousness which develops, it is the manifestation of consciousness which develops, its expression: it expresses itself more and more."

On "The Evolution of the Spiritual Man"

to be altogether unconscious.

It is the appearance that is inconscient. It becomes more and more conscious. Even in the mineral kingdom there are phenomena which reveal a hidden consciousness, like certain crystals, for instance. If you see with what precision, what exactitude and harmony they are formed, if you are in the least open, you are bound to feel that behind there's a consciousness at work, that this cannot be the result of unconscious chance.

Have you seen rock-crystals?... You have never seen a rock-crystal?

Yes.

It is pretty, isn't it? It is something very artistic.

And the movements of the sea, the movements of the air, of the wind, one can't help feeling that behind there is a consciousness or even many consciousnesses at work. In fact, it is like that. Only the most superficial appearance is inconscient.

(*Silence*)

Is that all?

Indeed, in every being, the whole process of evolution is reproduced, as if at a dizzy speed one were reviewing all that has been done, and as if it were necessary to relive all that in a flash before taking the next step.

(*Silence*)

148   On "The Life Divine"

The start, the great journey in the inconscience, in darkness, oblivion, unconsciousness, the awakening... and the return to the light.

14 May 1958

"*As plant-life contains in itself the obscure possibility of the conscious animal, as the animal-mind is astir with the movements of feeling and perception and the rudiments of conception that are the first ground for man the thinker, so man the mental being is sublimated by the endeavour of the evolutionary Energy to develop out of him the spiritual man, the fully conscious being, man exceeding his first material self and discoverer of his true self and highest nature.*

"*But if this is to be accepted as the intention in Nature, there are two questions that put themselves at once and call for a definitive answer, — first, the exact nature of the transition from mental to spiritual being and, when that is given, the process and method of the evolution of the spiritual out of the mental man. It would at first sight seem evident that as each gradation emerges not only out of its precedent grade but in it, as Life emerges in Matter and is largely limited and determined in its self-expression by its material conditions, as Mind emerges in Life-in-Matter and is similarly limited and determined in its self-expression by life-conditions and material conditions, so Spirit too must emerge in a Mind embodied in Life-in-Matter and must be largely limited and determined by the*

> *mental conditions in which it has its roots as well as the life-conditions, the material conditions of its existence here....*"
> The Life Divine, SABCL, Vol. 19, pp. 851-52

As the beginnings of the supramental life, which must be the next realisation in the unfolding of the universe, develop, perhaps not in a very obvious way but very surely, it becomes more and more obvious that the most difficult way to approach this supramental life is intellectual activity.

It could be said that it is much more difficult to pass from the mental to the supramental life than to pass from a certain psychic emotion in life — something that is like a reflection, a luminous emanation of the divine Presence in matter — to the supramental consciousness; it is much easier to pass from that into the supramental consciousness than to pass from the highest intellectual speculation to any supramental vibration. Perhaps it is the word that misleads us! Perhaps it is because we call it "supramental" that we expect to reach it through a higher intellectual mental activity? But the fact is very different. With this very high, very pure, very noble intellectual activity, one seems to move towards a kind of cold, powerless abstraction, a frozen, an icy light which is surely very remote from life and still further away from the experience of the supramental reality. In this new substance which is spreading and acting in the world, there is a warmth, a power, a joy so intense that all intellectual activity seems cold and dry beside it. And

On "The Evolution of the Spiritual Man"

that is why the less one talks about these things the better it is. A single moment, a single impulse of deep and true love, an instant of the understanding which lies in the divine Grace brings you much closer to the goal than all possible explanations. Even a kind of refined sensation, subtle, clear, luminous, acute, which penetrates deep, opens the door for you more than the subtlest explanations.

And if we carry the experience still further, it seems that when one comes to the work of transformation of the body, when some cells of the body, more ready than others, more refined, more subtle, more plastic, are able to feel concretely the presence of the divine Grace, the divine Will, the divine Power, this Knowledge that is not intellectual but a knowledge by identity, when one feels this in the cells of the body, then the experience is so total, so imperative, so living, concrete, tangible, real that everything else seems a vain dream.

And so we may say that it is truly when the circle is complete and the two extremities touch, when the highest manifests in the most material, that the experience will be truly conclusive.

It seems that one can never truly understand until one understands with one's body.

21 May 1958

Sweet Mother, what does "mental honesty" mean exactly?

It is a mind that does not attempt to deceive itself. And in fact it is not an "attempt", for it succeeds very well in doing it!

It would seem that in the ordinary psychological constitution of man, the almost constant function of the mind is to give an acceptable explanation of what goes on in the "desire being", the vital, the most material parts of the mind and the subtlest parts of the body. There is a kind of general complicity in all the parts of the being to give an explanation and even a comfortable justification for everything we do, in order to avoid as far as possible the painful impressions left by the mistakes we commit and undesirable movements. For instance, unless one has undergone or taken up a special training, whatever one does, the mind gives itself a favourable enough explanation of it, so that one is not troubled. Only under the pressure of outer reactions or circumstances or movements coming from other people, does one gradually consent to look less favourably at what one is and does, and begins to ask oneself whether things could not be better than they are. Spontaneously, the first movement is what is known as self-defense. One puts oneself on one's guard and quite spontaneously one wants a justification... for the smallest things, absolutely

On "The Evolution of the Spiritual Man" 153

insignificant things — it is a normal attitude in life.

And explanations — one gives them to oneself; it is only under the pressure of circumstances that one begins to give them to others or to another, but first one makes oneself very comfortable; first thing: "It was like that, for it had to be like that, and it happened because of this, and...", and it is always the fault of circumstances or other people. And it truly requires an effort — unless, as I say, one has undergone a discipline, has acquired the habit of doing it automatically — it requires an effort to begin to understand that perhaps things are not like this, that perhaps one has not done exactly what one ought to have done or reacted as one should. And even when one begins to see it, a much greater effort is needed to recognise it... officially.

When one begins to see that one has made a mistake, the first movement of the mind is to push it into the background and to put a cloak in front of it, the cloak of a very fine little explanation, and as long as one is not obliged to show it, one hides it. And this is what I call "lack of mental honesty".

First, one deceives oneself by habit, but even when one begins not to deceive oneself, instinctively there is a movement of trying, trying to deceive oneself in order to feel comfortable. And so a still greater step is necessary once one has understood that one was deceiving oneself, to confess frankly, "Yes, I was deceiving myself."

All these things are so habitual, so automatic, as it were, that you are not even aware of them; but when you begin to want to establish some discipline over your being, you make discoveries which are really tremendously interesting. When you have discovered this, you become aware that you are living constantly in a... the best word is "self-deception", a state of wilful deceit; that is, you deceive yourself spontaneously. It is not that you need to reflect: spontaneously you put a pretty cloak over what you have done so that it doesn't show its true colours... and all this for things which are so insignificant, which have so little importance! It would be understandable, wouldn't it, if recognising your mistake had serious consequences for your very existence — the instinct of self-preservation would make you do it as a protection — but that is not the question, it concerns things which are absolutely unimportant, of no consequence at all except that of having to tell yourself, "I have made a mistake."

This means that an effort is needed in order to be mentally sincere. There must be an effort, there must be a discipline. Of course, I am not speaking of those who tell lies in order not to be caught, for everybody knows that this should not be done. Besides, the most stupid lies are the most useless, for they are so flagrant that they can't deceive anyone. Such examples occur constantly; you catch someone doing something wrong and tell him, "That's how it is"; he gives a silly explanation which nobody can understand, nobody can accept; it is silly but he gives it in the hope of shielding himself. It is spontaneous, you see, but he knows this is not done. But the other kind of deception is much more spontaneous and it is so habitual that one is not aware

On "The Evolution of the Spiritual Man"

of it. So, when we speak of mental honesty, we speak of something which is acquired by a very constant and sustained effort.

You catch yourself, don't you, you suddenly catch yourself in the act of giving yourself somewhere in your head or here (*Mother indicates the heart*), here it is more serious... giving a very favourable little explanation. And only when you can get a grip on yourself, there, hold fast and look at yourself clearly in the face and say, "Do you think it is like that?", then, if you are very courageous and put a very strong pressure, in the end you tell yourself, "Yes, I know very well that it is not like that!"

It sometimes takes years. Time must pass, one must have changed much within oneself, one's vision of things must have become different, one must be in a different condition, in a different relation with circumstances, in order to see clearly, completely, how far one was deceiving oneself — and at that moment one was convinced that one was sincere.

(*Silence*)

It is probable that perfect sincerity can only come when one rises above this sphere of falsehood that is life as we know it on earth, mental life, even the higher mental life.

When one springs up into the higher sphere, into the world of Truth, one will be able to see things as they truly are, and seeing them as they are, one will be able to live them in their truth. Then all falsehoods will naturally crumble. And since the favourable explanations will no longer have any purpose, they will disappear, for there will be nothing left to explain.

Things will be self-evident, Truth will shine through all forms, the possibility of error will disappear.

28 May 1958

"It is quite true that to a surface view Life seems only an operation of Matter, Mind an activity of Life, and it might seem to follow that what we call the soul or spirit is only a power of mentality, soul a fine form of Mind, spirituality a high activity of the embodied mental being. But this is a superficial view of things due to the thought's concentrating on the appearance and process and not looking at what lies behind the process. One might as well on the same lines have concluded that electricity is only a product or operation of water and cloud matter, because it is in such a field that lightning emerges; but a deeper inquiry has shown that both cloud and water have, on the contrary, the energy of electricity as their foundation, their constituent power or energysubstance: that which seems to be a result is, — in its reality, though not in its form, — the origin; the effect is in the essence pre-existent to the apparent cause, the principle of the emergent activity precedent to its present field of action. So it is throughout evolutionary Nature; Matter could not have become animate if the principle of Life had not been there constituting Matter and emerging as a phenomenon of Life-in-Matter; Life-in-Matter could not have begun to feel, perceive, think, reason, if the principle of Mind had not been there behind life and substance, constituting it as its field

> *of operation and emergent in the phenomenon of a thinking life and body: so too spirituality emerging in Mind is the sign of a power which itself has founded and constituted life, mind and body and is now emerging as a spiritual being in a living and thinking body. How far this emergence will go, whether it will become dominant and transform its instrument, is a subsequent question; but what is necessary first to posit is the existence of Spirit as something else than Mind and greater than Mind, spirituality as something other than mentality and the spiritual being therefore as something distinct from the mental being: Spirit is a final evolutionary emergence because it is the original involutionary element and factor. Evolution is an inverse action of the involution: what is an ultimate and last derivation in the involution is the first to appear in the evolution; what was original and primal in the involution is in the evolution the last and supreme emergence."*
>
> *The Life Divine*, SABCL, Vol. 19, pp. 852-53

Today I have been asked to speak to you about the Avatar.

The first thing I have to say is that Sri Aurobindo has written on this subject and the person who has asked me the question would do well to begin by reading what Sri Aurobindo has written.

I shall not speak to you about that, for it is better to read it for yourself.

On "The Evolution of the Spiritual Man" 159

But I could speak to you of a very old tradition, more ancient than the two known lines of spiritual and occult tradition, that is, the Vedic and Chaldean lines; a tradition which seems to have been at the origin of these two known traditions, in which it is said that when, as a result of the action of the adverse forces — known in the Hindu tradition as the Asuras — the world, instead of developing according to its law of Light and inherent consciousness, was plunged into the darkness, inconscience and ignorance that we know, the Creative Power implored the Supreme Origin, asking him for a special intervention which could save this corrupted universe; and in reply to this prayer there was emanated from the Supreme Origin a special Entity, of Love and Consciousness, who cast himself directly into the most inconscient matter to begin there the work of awakening it to the original Consciousness and Love.

In the old narratives this Being is described as stretched out in a deep sleep at the bottom of a very dark cave, and in his sleep there emanated from him prismatic rays of light which gradually spread into the Inconscience and embedded themselves in all the elements of this Inconscience to begin there the work of Awakening.

If one consciously enters into this Inconscient, one can still see there this same marvellous Being, still in deep sleep, continuing his work of emanation, spreading his Light; and he will continue to do it until the Inconscience is no longer inconscient, until Darkness disappears from the world — and the whole creation awakens to the Supramental Consciousness.

And it is remarkable that this wonderful Being strangely resembles the one whom I saw in vision one day, the Being who is at the other extremity, at the confines of form and the Formless. But that one was in a golden, crimson glory, whereas in his sleep the other Being was of a shining diamond whiteness emanating opalescent rays.

In fact, this is the origin of all Avatars. He is, so to say, the first universal Avatar who, gradually, has assumed more and more conscious bodies and finally manifested in a kind of recognised line of Beings who have descended directly from the Supreme to perfect this work of preparing the universe so that, through a continuous progression, it may become ready to receive and manifest the supramental Light in its entirety.

In every country, every tradition, the event has been presented in a special way, with different limitations, different details, particular features, but truly speaking, the origin of all these stories is the same, and that is what we could call a direct, conscious intervention of the Supreme in the darkest matter, without going through all the intermediaries, in order to awaken this Matter to the receptivity of the Divine Forces.

The intervals separating these various incarnations seem to become shorter and shorter, as if, to the extent that Matter became more and more ready, the action could accelerate and become more and more rapid in its movement, more and more conscious too, more and more effective and decisive.

And it will go on multiplying and intensifying until the entire universe becomes the total Avatar of the Supreme.

4 June 1958

"At first this truth of the spirit and of spirituality is not self-evident to the mind; man becomes mentally aware of his soul as something other than his body, superior to his normal mind and life, but he has no clear sense of it, only a feeling of some of its effects on his nature. As these effects take a mental form or a life-form, the difference is not firmly and trenchantly drawn, the soul-perception does not acquire a distinct and assured independence. Very commonly indeed, a complex of half-effects of the psychic pressure on the mental and vital parts, a formation mixed with mental aspiration and vital desires, is mistaken for the soul, just as the separative ego is taken for the self, although the self in its true being is universal as well as individual in its essence, — or just as a mixture of mental aspiration and vital enthusiasm and ardour uplifted by some kind of strong or high belief or self-dedication or altruistic eagerness is mistaken for spirituality. But this vagueness and these confusions are inevitable as a temporary stage of the evolution which, because ignorance is its starting-point and the whole stamp of our first nature, must necessarily begin with an imperfect intuitive perception and an instinctive urge or seeking without any acquired experience or clear knowledge. Even the formations which are the first effects of the perception or urge or the first

On "The Evolution of the Spiritual Man"

indices of a spiritual evolution, must inevitably be of this incomplete and tentative nature. But the error so created comes very much in the way of a true understanding, and it must therefore be emphasised that spirituality is not a high intellectuality, not idealism, not an ethical turn of mind or moral purity and austerity, not religiosity or an ardent and exalted emotional fervour, not even a compound of all these excellent things; a mental belief, creed or faith, an emotional aspiration, a regulation of conduct according to a religious or ethical formula are not spiritual achievement and experience. These things are of considerable value to mind and life; they are of value to the spiritual evolution itself as preparatory movements disciplining, purifying or giving a suitable form to the nature; but they still belong to the mental evolution, — the beginning of a spiritual realisation, experience, change is not yet there. Spirituality is in its essence an awakening to the inner reality of our being, to a spirit, self, soul which is other than our mind, life and body, an inner aspiration to know, to feel, to be that, to enter into contact with the greater Reality beyond and pervading the universe which inhabits also our own being, to be in communion with It and union with It, and a turning, a conversion, a transformation of our whole being as a result of the aspiration, the contact, the union, a growth or waking into a new becoming or new being, a new self, a new nature."

The Life Divine, SABCL, Vol. 19, pp. 856-57

In fact, so long as there is any doubt or hesitation, so long as one asks oneself the question of whether one has or hasn't realised this eternal soul in oneself, it proves that the *true* contact has not taken place. For, when the phenomenon occurs, it brings with it an inexpressible something, so new and so definitive, that doubt and questioning are no longer possible. It is truly, in the absolute sense of the phrase, a new birth.

You become a new person, and whatever may be the path or the difficulties of the path afterwards, that feeling never leaves you. It is not even something — like many other experiences — which withdraws, passes into the background, leaving you externally with a kind of vague memory to which it is difficult to cling, whose remembrance grows faint, blurred — it is not that. You are a new person and definitively that, whatever happens. And even all the incapacity of the mind, all the difficulties of the vital, all the inertia of the physical are unable to change this new state — a new state which makes a *decisive* break in the life of the consciousness. The being one was before and the being one is after, are no longer the same. The position one has in the universe and in relation to it, in life and in relation to it, in understanding and in relation to it, is no longer the same: it is a true reversal which can never be undone again. That is why when people tell me, "I would like to know whether I am in contact with my soul or not", I say, "If you ask the question, that is enough to prove that you are not. You don't need an answer, you are giving it to yourself." When it is *that*, it is that, and then it is

On "The Evolution of the Spiritual Man"

finished, it is no longer anything else.

And since we are speaking of that, I shall remind you of what Sri Aurobindo has said, repeated, written, affirmed and said over and over again, that his yoga, the integral yoga, can begin *only after* that experience, not before.

So, one must not cherish any illusions and fancy that one can begin to know what the supermind is and form any idea of it or assess it in any way, however minimal, before having had *that* experience.

Therefore, if you want to advance on the path, you must very modestly start on your way towards the new birth, first, and realise it before cherishing the illusion that you can have supramental experiences.

To console you I may tell you that by the very fact that you live on earth at this time — whether you are conscious of it or not, even whether you want it or not — you are absorbing with the air you breathe this new supramental substance which is now spreading in the earth atmosphere. And it is preparing things in you which will manifest *very suddenly*, as soon as you have taken the decisive step.

(*Silence*)

Whether this will help you to take the decisive step or not is another question which remains to be studied, for the experiences which are occurring and will occur more and more frequently now, being of a radically new kind, we can't know beforehand what is going to happen; we must study, and after a thorough study we shall be able to say with certainty whether this supramental substance makes the work of new birth easier or not.... I shall tell you this a little later. For the moment it is better not to rely on these things and, very simply, to start on your way to be born into the spiritual life.

When this happens to you, almost all the questions you ask yourself or ask me will be solved. And anyway, your attitude to life will be so different that you will understand what is meant when one speaks of living spiritually. And at that moment you will also understand a great thing, a very great thing: how to live without ego.

Until then, you cannot understand it. The whole of life is so dependent on the ego that it seems absolutely impossible to live and act except with or by the ego, but after this new birth you can look at the ego with a smile and say to it, "My friend, I don't need you any more."

This is also one of the results which brings you a very decisive sense of liberation.

11 June 1958

> *"When there is the decisive emergence, one sign of it is the status or action in us of an inherent, intrinsic, self-existent consciousness which knows itself by the mere fact of being, knows all that is in itself in the same way, by identity with it, begins even to see all that to our mind seems external in the same manner, by a movement of identity or by an intrinsic direct consciousness which envelops, penetrates, enters into its object, discovers itself in the object, is aware in it of something that is not mind or life or body. There is, then, evidently a spiritual consciousness which is other than the mental, and it testifies to the existence of a spiritual being in us which is other than our surface mental personality."*
>
> The Life Divine, SABCL, Vol. 19, p. 855

Sweet Mother, is there a spiritual being in everybody?

That depends on what we call "being". If for "being" we substitute "presence", yes, there is a spiritual presence in everyone. If we call "being" an organised entity, fully conscious of itself, independent, and having the power of asserting itself and ruling the rest of the nature — no! The possibility of this independent and all-powerful being is in everybody, but the realisation is the result of long efforts which sometimes extend over many lives.

In everyone, even at the very beginning, this spiritual presence, this inner light is there.... In fact, it is everywhere. I have seen it many a time in certain animals. It is like a shining point which is the basis of a certain control and protection, something which, even in half-consciousness, makes possible a certain harmony with the rest of creation so that irreparable catastrophes may not be constant and general. Without this presence the disorder created by the violences and passions of the vital would be so great that at any moment they could bring about a general catastrophe, a sort of total destruction which would prevent the progress of Nature. That presence, that spiritual light — which could almost be called a spiritual consciousness — is within each being and all things, and because of it, in spite of all discordance, all passion, all violence, there is a minimum of general harmony which allows Nature's work to be accomplished.

And this presence becomes quite obvious in the human being, even the most rudimentary. Even in the most monstrous human being, in one who gives the impression of being an incarnation of a devil or a monster, there is something within exercising a sort of irresistible control — even in the worst, some things are impossible. And without this presence, if the being were controlled exclusively by the adverse forces, the forces of the vital, this impossibility would not exist.

Each time a wave of these monstrous adverse forces sweeps over the earth, one feels that nothing can ever stop the disorder and horror from spreading, and always, at a certain time, unexpectedly and inexplicably a control intervenes, and the wave is arrested, the catastrophe is not total. And this is because of the Presence, the supreme Presence, in matter.

But only in a few exceptional beings and after a long, very long work of preparation extending over many, many lives does this Presence change into a conscious, independent, fully organised being, all-powerful master of his dwelling-place, conscious enough, powerful enough, to be able to control not only this dwelling but what surrounds it and in a field of radiation and action that is more and more extensive... and effective.

18 June 1958

"There are four main lines which Nature has followed in her attempt to open up the inner being, — religion, occultism, spiritual thought and an inner spiritual realisation and experience: the three first are approaches, the last is the decisive avenue of entry. All these four powers have worked by a simultaneous action, more or less connected, sometimes in a variable collaboration, sometimes in dispute with each other, sometimes in a separate independence. Religion has admitted an occult element in its ritual, ceremony, sacraments; it has leaned upon spiritual thinking, deriving from it sometimes a creed or theology, sometimes its supporting spiritual philosophy, — the former, ordinarily, is the occidental method, the latter the oriental: but spiritual experience is the final aim and achievement of religion, its sky and summit. But also religion has sometimes banned occultism or reduced its own occult element to a minimum; it has pushed away the philosophic mind as a dry intellectual alien, leaned with all its weight on creed and dogma, pietistic emotion and fervour and moral conduct; it has reduced to a minimum or dispensed with spiritual realisation and experience. Occultism has sometimes put forward a spiritual aim as its goal, and followed occult knowledge and experience as an approach to it, formulated some kind of mystic philosophy: but more often it has

confined itself to occult knowledge and practice without any spiritual vistas; it has turned to thaumaturgy or mere magic or even deviated into diabolism. Spiritual philosophy has very usually leaned on religion as its support or its way to experience; it has been the outcome of realisation and experience or built its structures as an approach to it: but it has also rejected all aid, — or all impediment, — of religion and proceeded in its own strength, either satisfied with mental knowledge or confident to discover its own path of experience and effective discipline. Spiritual experience has used all the three means as a starting-point, but it has also dispensed with them all, relying on its own pure strength: discouraging occult knowledge and powers as dangerous lures and entangling obstacles, it has sought only the pure truth of the spirit; dispensing with philosophy, it has arrived instead through the heart's fervour or a mystic inward spiritualisation; putting behind it all religious creed, worship and practice and regarding them as an inferior stage or first approach, it has passed on, leaving behind it all these supports, nude of all these trappings, to the sheer contact of the spiritual Reality. All these variations were necessary; the evolutionary endeavour of Nature has experimented on all lines in order to find her true way and her whole way towards the supreme consciousness and the integral knowledge.

"For each of these means or approaches corresponds to something in our total being and therefore

to something necessary to the total aim of her evolution. There are four necessities of man's self-expansion if he is not to remain this being of the surface ignorance seeking obscurely after the truth of things and collecting and systematising fragments and sections of knowledge, the small limited and half-competent creature of the cosmic Force which he now is in his phenomenal nature. He must know himself and discover and utilise all his potentialities: but to know himself and the world completely he must go behind his own and its exterior, he must dive deep below his own mental surface and the physical surface of Nature. This he can only do by knowing his inner mental, vital, physical and psychic being and its powers and movements and the universal laws and processes of the occult Mind and Life which stand behind the material front of the universe: that is the field of occultism, if we take the word in its widest significance. He must know also the hidden Power or Powers that control the world: if there is a Cosmic Self or Spirit or a Creator, he must be able to enter into relation with It or Him and be able to remain in whatever contact or communion is possible, get into some kind of tune with the master Beings of the universe or with the universal Being and its universal will or a supreme Being and His supreme will, follow the law It gives him and the assigned or revealed aim of his life and conduct, raise himself towards the highest height that It demands of him in his life now or in his existence hereafter; if there is no such universal or supreme Spirit or Being, he must know what there is and how to lift himself to it out of his present imperfection and impotence. This approach is the aim of religion: its purpose is to link the human with the Divine and in so doing sublimate the thought and life and flesh so that they may admit the rule of the soul and spirit. But this knowledge must be something more than a creed or a mystic revelation; his thinking mind must be able to accept it, to correlate it with the principle of things and the observed truth of the universe: this is the work of philosophy, and in the field of the truth of the spirit it can only be done by a spiritual philosophy, whether intellectual in its method or intuitive. But all knowledge and endeavour can reach its fruition only if it is turned into experience and has become a part of the consciousness and its established operations; in the spiritual field all this religious, occult or philosophical knowledge and endeavour must, to bear fruition, end in an opening up of the spiritual consciousness, in experiences that found and continually heighten, expand and enrich that consciousness and in the building of a life and action that is in conformity with the truth of the spirit: this is the work of spiritual realisation and experience."

The Life Divine, SABCL, Vol. 19, pp. 860-62

One point is very remarkable — I don't remember whether Sri Aurobindo speaks about it in what follows — but among the four activities or realisations he mentions — religion, occultism, spiritual philosophy and spiritual experience — which are necessary for the development and transformation of man, all are not equally accessible to humanity.

The one which can be practised and, one might say, "understood" — although it is certainly not an "understanding" — by the greatest number of human beings — those who live almost exclusively in the physical consciousness — is the religious method, precisely because it is based on fixed creeds and practices. Simply by an act of faith or a collective suggestion — above all a collective suggestion — many human beings who have not yet reached any considerable inner development can take up the path of religion.

For occultism we must already have come to a second stage of development and be more conscious in the vital world to be able to come into contact with the play of forces, which is indispensable in order to manipulate them.

As for spiritual philosophy, only the few who have a fairly complete mental development and are fully conscious on the intellectual plane, can usefully adopt this method; otherwise it is a dead letter for all those who don't have an ability for mental gymnastics and so cannot follow all the acrobatics of the mind.

And finally, Sri Aurobindo has told us somewhere in *The Life Divine* that to follow the path of spiritual experience, one must have within oneself a "spiritual being", one must be "twice born" as it is said, for if one

On "The Evolution of the Spiritual Man"   175

doesn't have a spiritual being within, which is at least on the point of becoming self-aware, one may try to imitate these experiences but it will only be crude imitation or hypocrisy, it won't be a reality.

Therefore, in order to follow these four paths simultaneously and to practise them with an integral benefit for the being, one must already be a complete individual, capable of having a conscious life in the four principal elements of human and spiritual nature.

Of course, this inner development is not always apparent and we may meet someone who has within him a conscious spiritual entity, ready for the most beautiful experiences, though externally he seems quite crude and incomplete.

Nor is it necessary to follow this development in the order in which it has been mentioned, but if we want our realisation to be integral and to arrive at a total transformation of our being, we must be able to use the essence of what each of these methods can bring.

The psychic or spiritual consciousness gives you the deep inner realisation, contact with the Divine, liberation from external fetters; but for this liberation to be effective, for it to have an action on the rest of the being, the mind must be open enough to be able to hold the spiritual light of Knowledge, the vital must be powerful enough to handle the forces behind appearances and dominate them, and the physical should be disciplined, organised enough to be able to *express* the deep experience, in the movements of each day and each moment, and live it integrally.

If one of these things is lacking, the result is not complete. One can make light of this thing or that under the pretext that it is not the most important, the central Thing — and to neglect outer things certainly cannot prevent you from entering into spiritual communion with the Supreme, but that is good only for a flight from life.

If we are to be total, complete beings, to have an integral realisation, we should be able to express our spiritual experience mentally, vitally and physically. And the more our expression is perfect, executed by a complete and perfect being, the more integral and perfect will our realisation be.

For someone who wants to follow the integral yoga nothing is useless and nothing must be neglected.... The main thing is to know how to put each thing in its place and to hand over the government to what truly has the right to govern.

25 June 1958

"In the very nature of things all evolution must proceed at first by a slow unfolding; for each new principle that evolves its powers has to make its way out of an involution in Inconscience and Ignorance. It has a difficult task in pulling itself out of the involution, out of the hold of the obscurity of the original medium, against the pull and strains, the instinctive opposition and obstruction of the Inconscience and the hampering mixture and blind obstinate retardations of the Ignorance. Nature affirms at first a vague urge and tendency which is a sign of the push of the occult, subliminal, submerged reality towards the surface; there are then small half-suppressed hints of the thing that is to be, imperfect beginnings, crude elements, rudimentary appearances, small, insignificant, hardly recognisable quanta. Afterwards there are small or large formations; a more characteristic and recognisable quality begins to show itself, first partially, here and there or in a low intensity, then more vivid, more formative; finally, there is the decisive emergence, a reversal of the consciousness, the beginning of the possibility of its radical change: but still much has to be done in every direction, a long and difficult growth towards perfection lies before the evolutionary endeavour. The thing done has not only to be confirmed, secured against relapse

and the downward gravitation, against failure and extinction, but opened out into all the fields of its possibilities, its totality of entire self-achievement, its utmost height, subtlety, riches, wideness; it has to become dominant, all-embracing, comprehensive. This is everywhere the process of Nature and to ignore it is to miss the intention in her works and get lost in the maze of her procedure."

The Life Divine, SABCL, Vol. 19, pp. 862-63

This seems to be a very exact description of individual development. It is exactly like that. And so you lose patience or lose courage, for you feel that you are not advancing. But when you engage in the development of the body — material, physical development — when you want the physical body to do sadhana, it is exactly like that. You begin by trying out all kinds of things without precision or exactitude, without knowing which end to begin with, and you feel you are groping, searching, going round and round and going nowhere. And then, gradually, one thing comes up and then another, and it is only very much later that something like a programme begins to be worked out. And this description Sri Aurobindo gives at the end, when the goal of evolution emerges and becomes perceptible, how much care must be taken for it not to be engulfed once again in the primal Inconscience!

And that is why the work seems... interminable. And yet this is the only way it can be done. The road to be covered between the usual state of the body, the almost total inconscience to which we are accustomed because we are "like that", and the perfect awakening of consciousness, the response of all the cells, all the organs, all the functionings... between the two there seem to be centuries of labour. However, if one has learnt to open, to aspire, give oneself up, and if one can make use of these same movements in the body, teach the cells to do the same thing, then things go much faster. But much faster does not mean fast; it is still a long and slow work. And each time that an element which has not entered the movement of transformation wakes up to enter it, one feels that everything must be started again — all that one believed had been done must be done once more. But it is not true, it is not the same thing that one does again, it is something similar in a new element which was either forgotten or else left aside because it was not ready, and which, now that it is ready, awakens and wants to take its place. There are many elements like that....

The body seems to you to be something very simple, doesn't it? It is a body, it is "my" body, and after all it has a single form — but it is not like that! There are hundreds of combined entities unaware of each other, all harmonised by something deeper which they do not know, and having a perception of unity only because they are not conscious of the multiplicity of the elements and their divergence.

In fact, this multiplicity and divergence are the cause of most disorders and even illnesses. Something is going well, you have caught the guiding thread, you are following your path, you think you are going to get a result, and then, suddenly, there! — something happens quite unexpectedly, you did not know it was there: it wakes up and insists on joining the march. But it creates a terrible disorder and you must begin everything over again.

The sadhana of all the inner beings, inner domains, has been done by many people, has been explained at length, systematised by some, the stages and paths have been traced out and you go from one stage to another, knowing that it has to be like that; but as soon as you go down into the body, it is like a virgin forest.... And everything is to be done, everything is to be worked out, everything is to be built up. So you must arm yourself with *great* patience, great patience, and not think that you are good for nothing because it takes so much time. You must never be despondent, never tell yourself, "Oh! This is not for me!" Everyone can do it, if he puts into it the time, the courage, the endurance and the perseverance that are demanded. But all this is needed. And above all, above all, never lose heart, be ready to begin the same thing again ten times, twenty times, a hundred times — until it is really done.

And one often feels that unless *everything* is done, unless the work is finished, well, it is as if one had done nothing.

9 July 1958

"Religion has opened itself to denial by its claim to determine the truth by divine authority, by inspiration, by a sacrosanct and infallible sovereignty given to it from on high; it has sought to impose itself on human thought, feeling, conduct without discussion or question. This is an excessive and premature claim, although imposed in a way on the religious idea by the imperative and absolute character of the inspirations and illuminations which are its warrant and justification and by the necessity of faith as an occult light and power from the soul amidst the mind's ignorance, doubts, weakness, incertitudes. Faith is indispensable to man, for without it he could not proceed forward in his journey through the Unknown; but it ought not to be imposed, it should come as a free perception or an imperative direction from the inner spirit. A claim to unquestioned acceptance could only be warranted if the spiritual effort had already achieved man's progression to the highest Truth-Consciousness total and integral, free from all ignorant mental and vital mixture. This is the ultimate object before us, but it has not yet been accomplished, and the premature claim has obscured the true work of the religious instinct in man, which is to lead him towards the Divine Reality, to formulate all that he has yet achieved in that direction and to give to each human being a mould

of spiritual discipline, a way of seeking, touching, nearing the Divine Truth, a way which is proper to the potentialities of his nature."
                The Life Divine, SABCL, Vol. 19, pp. 863-64

Sweet Mother, can faith be increased by personal effort?

Faith is certainly a gift given to us by the Divine Grace. It is like a door suddenly opening upon an eternal truth, through which we can see it, almost touch it.

As in everything else in the ascent of humanity, there is the necessity — especially at the beginning — of personal effort. It is possible that in some exceptional circumstances, for reasons which completely elude our intelligence, faith may come almost accidentally, quite unexpectedly, almost without ever having been solicited, but most frequently it is an answer to a yearning, a need, an aspiration, something in the being that is seeking and longing, even though not in a very conscious and systematic way. But in any case, when faith has been granted, when one has had this sudden inner illumination, in order to preserve it constantly in the active consciousness individual effort is altogether indispensable. One must *hold* on to one's faith, will one's faith; one must seek it, cultivate it, protect it.

In the human mind there is a morbid and deplorable habit of doubt, argument, scepticism. This is where human effort must be put in: the refusal to admit them, the refusal to listen to them and still more the refusal to follow them. No game is more dangerous than playing mentally with doubt and scepticism. They are not only enemies, they are terrible pitfalls, and once one falls into them, it becomes tremendously difficult to pull oneself out.

Some people think it is a very great mental elegance to play with ideas, to discuss them, to contradict their faith; they think that this gives them a very superior attitude, that in this way they are above "superstitions" and "ignorance"; but if you listen to suggestions of doubt and scepticism, *then* you fall into the grossest ignorance and stray away from the right path. You enter into confusion, error, a maze of contradictions.... You are not always sure you will be able to get out of it. You go so far away from the inner truth that you lose sight of it and sometimes lose too all possible contact with your soul.

Certainly a personal effort is needed to preserve one's faith, to let it grow within. Later — much later — one day, looking back, we may see that everything that happened, even what seemed to us the worst, was a Divine Grace to make us advance on the way; and then we become aware that the personal effort too was a grace. But before reaching that point, one has to advance much, to struggle much, sometimes even to suffer a great deal.

To sit down in inert passivity and say, "If I am to have faith I shall have it, the Divine will give it to me", is an attitude of laziness, of unconsciousness and almost of bad-will.

For the inner flame to burn, one must feed it; one must watch over the fire, throw into it the fuel of all the errors one wants to get rid of, all that delays the progress, all that darkens the path. If one doesn't feed the fire, it smoulders under the ashes of one's unconsciousness and inertia, and then, not years but lives, centuries will pass before one reaches the goal.

One must watch over one's faith as one watches over the birth of something *infinitely* precious, and protect it very carefully from everything that can impair it.

In the ignorance and darkness of the beginning, faith is the most direct expression of the Divine Power which comes to fight and conquer.

16 July 1958

"Religion's real business is to prepare man's mind, life and bodily existence for the spiritual consciousness to take it up; it has to lead him to that point where the inner spiritual light begins fully to emerge. It is at this point that religion must learn to subordinate itself, not to insist on its outer characters, but give full scope to the inner spirit itself to develop its own truth and reality. In the meanwhile it has to take up as much of man's mentality, vitality, physicality as it can and give all his activities a turn towards the spiritual direction, the revelation of a spiritual meaning in them, the imprint of a spiritual refinement, the beginning of a spiritual character. It is in this attempt that the errors of religion come in, for they are caused by the very nature of the matter with which it is dealing, — that inferior stuff invades the very forms that are meant to serve as intermediaries between the spiritual and the mental, vital or physical consciousness, and often it diminishes, degrades and corrupts them: but it is in this attempt that lies religion's greatest utility as an intercessor between spirit and nature. Truth and error live always together in the human evolution and the truth is not to be rejected because of its accompanying errors, though these have to be eliminated, — often a difficult business and, if crudely done, resulting in surgical harm inflicted on the body of religion; for

> *what we see as error is very frequently the symbol or a disguise or a corruption or malformation of a truth which is lost in the brutal radicality of the operation, — the truth is cut out along with the error. Nature herself very commonly permits the good corn and the tares and weeds to grow together for a long time, because only so is her own growth, her free evolution possible."*
>
> *The Life Divine*, SABCL, Vol. 19, pp. 864-65

Sweet Mother, is religion a necessity in the life of the ordinary man?

In the life of societies it is a necessity, for it serves as a corrective to collective egoism which, without this control, could take on excessive proportions.

The level of collective consciousness is always lower than the individual level. It is very noticeable, for example, that when men gather in a group or collect in great numbers, the level of consciousness falls a great deal. The consciousness of crowds is much lower than individual consciousness, and the collective consciousness of society is certainly lower than the consciousness of the individuals constituting it.

There it is a necessity. In ordinary life, an individual, whether he knows it or not, always has a religion but the object of his religion is sometimes of a very inferior kind.... The god he worships may be the god of success or the god of money or the god of power, or simply a family god: the god of children, the god of the family,

On "The Evolution of the Spiritual Man"

the god of the ancestors. There is always a religion. The quality of the religion is very different according to the individual, but it is difficult for a human being to live and to go on living, to survive in life without having something like a rudiment of an ideal which serves as the *centre* for his existence. Most of the time he doesn't know it and if he were asked what his ideal is, he would be unable to formulate it; but he has one, vaguely, something that seems to him the most precious thing in life.

For most people, it is security, for instance: living in security, being in conditions where one is sure of being able to go on existing. That is one of the great "aims", one might say, one of the great motives of human effort. There are people for whom comfort is the important thing; for others it is pleasure, amusement.

All that is very low and one would not be inclined to give it the name of an ideal, but it is truly a form of religion, something which may seem to be worth consecrating one's life to.... There are many influences which seek to impose themselves on human beings by using that as a basis. The feeling of insecurity, uncertainty, is a kind of tool, a means used by political or religious groups to influence individuals. They play on these ideas.

Every political or social idea is a sort of lower expression of an ideal which is a rudimentary religion. As soon as there is a faculty of thought, there is necessarily an aspiration for something higher than the most brutal daily existence from minute to minute, and this is what gives the energy and possibility of living.

Of course, one could say that it is the same thing

for individuals as for collectivities, that their value is exactly proportionate to the value of their ideal, their religion, that is, of the thing they make the summit of their existence.

Of course, when we speak of religion, if we mean the recognised religions, truly, everyone has his own religion, whether he knows it or not, even when he belongs to the great religions that have a name and a history. It is certain that even if one learns the dogmas by heart and complies with a prescribed ritual, everybody understands and acts in his own way, and only the name of the religion is the same, but this same religion is not the same for all the individuals who think they are practising it.

We can say that without some expression of this aspiration for the Unknown and the highest, human existence would be very difficult. If there were not at the heart of every being the hope of something better — of whatever kind — he would have difficulty in finding the energy needed to go on living.

(*Silence*)

But as very few individuals are capable of thinking freely, it is much easier to join a religion, accept it, adopt it and become a part of that religious collectivity than to formulate one's own cult for oneself. So, apparently, one is this or that, but in fact it is only an appearance.

23 July 1958

Mother, how can the faculty of intuition be developed?

There are different kinds of intuition, and we carry these capacities within us. They are always active to some extent but we don't notice them because we don't pay enough attention to what is going on in us.

Behind the emotions, deep within the being, in a consciousness seated somewhere near the level of the solar plexus, there is a sort of prescience, a kind of capacity for foresight, but not in the form of ideas: rather in the form of feelings, almost a perception of sensations. For instance, when one is going to decide to do something, there is sometimes a kind of uneasiness or inner refusal, and usually, if one listens to this deeper indication, one realises that it was justified.

In other cases there is something that urges, indicates, insists — I am not speaking of impulses, you understand, of all the movements which come from the vital and much lower still — indications which are behind the feelings, which come from the affective part of the being; there too one can receive a fairly sure indication of the thing to be done. These are forms of intuition or of a higher instinct which can be cultivated by observation and also by studying the results. Naturally, it must be done very sincerely, objectively, without prejudice. If one wants to see things in a particular way and at the same time practise this observation, it is all useless. One must do it as if one were looking at what is happening from outside oneself, in someone else.

It is one form of intuition and perhaps the first one that usually manifests.

There is also another form but that one is much more difficult to observe because for those who are accustomed to think, to act by reason — not by impulse but by reason — to reflect before doing anything, there is an extremely swift process from cause to effect in the half-conscious thought which prevents you from seeing the line, the whole line of reasoning and so you don't think that it is a chain of reasoning, and that is quite deceptive. You have the impression of an intuition but it is not an intuition, it is an extremely rapid subconscious reasoning, which takes up a problem and goes straight to the conclusions. This must not be mistaken for intuition.

In the ordinary functioning of the brain, intuition is something which suddenly falls like a drop of light. If one has the faculty, the beginning of a faculty of mental vision, it gives the impression of something coming from outside or above, like a little impact of a drop of light in the brain, absolutely independent of all reasoning.

This is perceived more easily when one is able to silence one's mind, hold it still and attentive, arresting its usual functioning, as if the mind were changed into a kind of mirror turned towards a higher faculty in a sustained and silent attention. That too one can learn to do. One must learn to do it, it is a necessary discipline.

When you have a question to solve, whatever it may be, usually you concentrate your attention here (*pointing between the eyebrows*), at the centre just above the eyes, the centre of the conscious will. But then if you do that, you cannot be in contact with intuition. You can be in contact with the source of the will, of effort, even of a certain kind of knowledge, but in the outer, almost material field; whereas, if you want to contact the intuition, you must keep this (*Mother indicates the forehead*) completely immobile. Active thought must be stopped as far as possible and the entire mental faculty must form — at the top of the head and a little further above if possible — a kind of mirror, very quiet, very still, turned upwards, in silent, very concentrated attention. If you succeed, you can — perhaps not immediately — but you can have the perception of the drops of light falling upon the mirror from a still unknown region and expressing themselves as a conscious thought which has no connection with all the rest of your thought since you have been able to keep it silent. That is the real beginning of the intellectual intuition.

It is a discipline to be followed. For a long time one may try and not succeed, but as soon as one succeeds in making a "mirror", still and attentive, one always obtains a result, not necessarily with a precise form of thought but always with the sensations of a light coming from above. And then, if one can receive this light coming from above without entering immediately into a whirl of activity, receive it in calm and silence and let it penetrate deep into the being, then after a while it expresses itself either as a luminous thought or as a very precise indication here (*Mother indicates the heart*), in this other centre.

Naturally, first these two faculties must be developed; then, as soon as there is any result, one must observe the result, as I said, and see the connection with what is happening, the consequences: see, observe very attentively what has come in, what may have caused a distortion, what one has added by way of more or less conscious reasoning or the intervention of a lower will, also more or less conscious; and it is by a very deep study — indeed, almost of every moment, in any case daily and very frequent — that one succeeds in developing one's intuition. It takes a long time. It takes a long time and there are ambushes: one can deceive oneself, take for intuitions subconscious wills which try to manifest, indications given by impulses one has refused to receive openly, indeed all sorts of difficulties. One must be prepared for that. But if one persists, one is sure to succeed.

And there comes a time when one feels a kind of inner guidance, something which is leading one very perceptibly in all that one does. But then, for the guidance to have its maximum power, one must naturally add to it a conscious surrender: one must be sincerely determined to follow the indication given by the higher force. If one does that, then... one saves years of study, one can seize the result extremely rapidly. If one also does that, the result comes very rapidly. But for that, it must be done with sincerity and... a kind of inner spontaneity.

On "The Evolution of the Spiritual Man"

If one wants to try without this surrender, one may succeed — as one can also succeed in developing one's personal will and making it into a very considerable power — but that takes a very long time and one meets many obstacles and the result is very precarious; one must be very persistent, obstinate, persevering, and one is sure to succeed, but only after a great labour.

Make your surrender with a sincere, complete self-giving, and you will go ahead at full speed, you will go much faster — but you must not do this calculatingly, for that spoils everything!

(*Silence*)

Moreover, whatever you may want to do in life, one thing is absolutely indispensable and at the basis of everything, the capacity of concentrating the attention. If you are able to gather together the rays of attention and consciousness on one point and can maintain this concentration with a persistent will, *nothing* can resist it — whatever it may be, from the most material physical development to the highest spiritual one. But this discipline must be followed in a constant and, it may be said, imperturbable way; not that you should always be concentrated on the same thing — that's not what I mean, I mean learning to concentrate.

And materially, for studies, sports, all physical or mental development, it is absolutely indispensable. And the value of an individual is proportionate to the value of his attention.

And from the spiritual point of view it is still more important. There is no spiritual obstacle which can resist a penetrating power of concentration. For instance, the discovery of the psychic being, union with the inner Divine, opening to the higher spheres, all can be obtained by an intense and obstinate power of concentration — but one must learn how to do it.

There is nothing in the human or even in the superhuman field, to which the power of concentration is not the key.

You can be the best athlete, you can be the best student, you can be an artistic, literary or scientific genius, you can be the greatest saint with that faculty. And everyone has in himself a tiny little beginning of it — it is given to everybody, but people do not cultivate it.

30 July 1958

Sweet Mother, what kind of forces can be called up by using the planchette, and how is it done?

Oh! Oh!... Do you mean automatic writing?

Yes, Mother.

That depends on the people who do it. Sometimes there are no forces at all! It is the mental and vital vibrations of the people who use the planchette, and it is their own subconscious ideas which they bring up, ninety-eight times out of a hundred.[1] If they are in contact with invisible entities, it may be all sorts of things but nothing very advisable!

Almost with certainty it could be said that it is not what people think it is, in the sense that most often they try to evoke what they call the "spirit" of a dead person, a relative or a friend or someone they loved and with whom they wish to remain in touch; and besides, they ask them the most foolish questions. Fortunately they don't succeed in disturbing them....

From this point of view one can say that if you had a relation of deep and sincere love with someone who

1. Later Mother added the following remark: "I say ninety times out of a hundred, for there are exceptions — I know of some — but they are so rare that it is better not to speak about them."

has passed away, left his body, and if you are calm and strong enough yourself, this person may choose to take shelter vitally in your atmosphere — the atmosphere of the one he loves — for a more or less long period. In this case it means that the relation was very close, very intimate, and if you are not altogether materialistic to the point of not having any direct mental perception, you can remain in mental contact with this person, in communication with him. It is a rather exceptional case, for usually if your atmosphere is calm and strong enough to be able to truly serve as a protection, the person who has left his body enters into a deep rest there, and it is not at all good to disturb it; and the best thing you can do is to enfold this person with your love and leave him in peace.

Therefore, even if it were possible to enter into communication with him by this means, which I would call very crude, it would be improper to do so. But usually, people who have the capacity, the faculties required to serve as a shelter for some time, a transitional shelter for those who have gone, do not have this ridiculous idea of disturbing the rest of the one they love by tapping on a planchette... fortunately!

But those who indulge in this exercise, an exercise of unhealthy curiosity, get what they deserve; for the atmosphere we live in is filled with a great number of small vital entities which are born of unsatisfied desires, vital movements of a very low type, also the decomposition of larger beings of the vital world; indeed, it is swarming with them, you see. It is surely a protection

On "The Evolution of the Spiritual Man" 197

that most people do not see what is going on in this vital atmosphere, for it is not especially pleasant; but if they have the presumption to want to come into contact with it and set about trying automatic writing or table-turning or... indeed, anything of this kind, out of an unhealthy curiosity, well, what happens is that one of these small entities or several of them have fun at their expense and collect all the necessary indications from their subconscious mind and then furnish these things to them as clear proofs that they are the person who has been called!

I could write a book for you with all the examples I have known of these stories, for people are very proud of doing things like this and immediately write them down, giving "proofs" of the truth of the experience which are so ridiculous that they should be enough to show them that someone was making fun of them! I had another instance, very recently, of somebody who fancied that he had entered into contact with Sri Aurobindo and was receiving sensational revelations from him — that was comical in the extreme.

But anyway, as a rule, it is — oh! most often — it is your own forces, your subconscious mental and vital forces which you put into the planchette — and you make sensational revelations to yourself! One can do many things in this way.... Once I wanted to prove to people that what they were evoking was nothing but themselves; so I had a little fun, simply with a concentration of the will, tapping the furniture, making tables walk and, well!... As for automatic writing, you only have to withdraw your conscious will into yourself, to let your hand go — just like this (*gesture*) — and leave it free, and then the hand will begin to make movements; but there is a little part in you which is interested and would like these movements to make sense and this little part appeals to the subconscious mind which begins to make sensational revelations. Indeed, it is a booby-trap, all this business, unless one does it scientifically — but then, scientifically, one realises that it leads to nothing, nothing at all except just passing your time in what you consider an interesting way.

In some cases vital entities really get hold of you, and there it is dangerous. But fortunately these cases are not very frequent. Then it becomes very dangerous.

A very long time ago when I was in France, I knew the case of a man who, through practices of this kind, had put himself into contact with a vital entity. This man happened to be a gambler and he spent his time speculating and playing roulette. He spent part of the year at Monte Carlo playing roulette and the rest of the time he lived in the south of France and speculated on the Stock Exchange. And now, some being was really using him — it was through automatic writing — using him, and for years it gave him absolutely precise, exact indications. When he played roulette it used to tell him, "Bid on this number or this place", and he would win. Naturally he just worshipped this "spirit" which gave him such sensational revelations. And at the Exchange it also told him, "Speculate on this or on that" and gave him all the indications. This man became colossally rich.

He used to boast to all his friends about the method by which he had grown rich.

Someone put him on his guard, told him, "Be careful, this doesn't look very honest, you should not trust this spirit." He fell out with this person. A few days later he was in Monte Carlo and... He always played for high stakes, you see; since, naturally, he always won and would break the bank, he was much feared. Then the spirit told him, "Stake everything, *everything* you have on this...." He did, and at a single stroke lost everything! And yet, he still had some money left from his Stock Exchange speculations. He said to himself, "It is bad luck." Again he received a very precise indication, "Do this", as usual. And he did it — he was completely cleaned out! And to finish the job, the spirit told him, just for the fun of it, "Now, you are going to commit suicide. Put a bullet through your head". And he was so much under its influence, he did so.... That's the end of the story. And this is an authentic story. So, the least one can say is that it is dangerous, it is much better not to indulge in occupations of this kind.

No! Either they are rather senseless amusements or else they are unwholesome occupations.

Mother, Sri Aurobindo wrote the book Yogic Sadhan in this way...

No, no! It is not that at all. You must not confuse things. That was something different. Sri Aurobindo knew with whom he was in contact, he did it deliberately and chose the person he was in touch with, and that had nothing to do with the little entities I am speaking about, nothing at all, at all. It was something that took place in the mental world, directly; you must not confuse things. This has no connection, none at all.

(*Silence*)

One can, if one has the knowledge, the control, the power, the ability to go into a certain state of passivity — one can very easily lend one's hand to someone, deliberately, knowing who it is and acting on a higher plane, but that already demands a great consciousness and a great self-mastery, which is not within everybody's reach. One must have quite a considerable inner development to be able to see whom one is dealing with on a particular plane and willingly lend oneself to the experiment with full knowledge of what one is doing and without losing one's control. Not everybody can play with that. But to work the planchette, one only has to delude oneself enough for it to start working!

What you are telling us now, Mother — does it form part of the occult sciences?

It was simply to make an experiment, that's all.

(*Silence*)

It is not a good way of approach, as a general rule, for in

the inner field, in the domain of inner development, this corresponds to the need to read novels. People whose minds are insufficiently developed, whose minds are still in a tamasic state and half inert, need to read novels in order to wake up. It is not the sign of a very commendable state or at any rate a very high one. Well, in the field of inner development this corresponds to the same thing. When one is in a very rudimentary state, when one has no intense inner life, one needs to read novels or to create novels for oneself, and then one indulges in experiments of this kind and believes one is doing very interesting things.... This has the same interest as novels — not even literary novels but cheap romances, those published on the back of newspapers.

Sri Aurobindo told me that some people needed this because their minds were so inert that this shook them and woke them up a little! Well, that is the same thing. Some people may need to do exercises of this kind to awaken their vital a little, which is sleepy and inert and... this gives them a little interest in life. But still, one can't say that these are very valuable occupations. They are pastimes, amusements.

And this has never served to prove anything to anybody. One could say, "Oh! It is to make you understand that there is an inner life, an invisible life, and it puts you in touch with things you don't see and proves to you that they exist". That is not true.

Unless you have a spiritual *being* within you, capable of awakening and living its own life, all these things teach you nothing at all. I knew some people — one of them especially, who was a man of science, intelligent, a man of real ability; he had studied higher science, become an engineer and held an important position; this man was a member of a society known as "spiritualist", which had found a medium who really had quite exceptional abilities. And he used to attend all the séances with the idea of learning, to convince himself and have tangible proofs of the existence of an invisible world, the concrete and real existence of an invisible world. He had seen all that could be seen, under the strictest control, in the most scientific way possible — all the tests were provided for, down to the least detail. He told me about the most extraordinary things he had seen; I held in my hand a piece of something resembling the plastic cloth they make nowadays, which is not woven, a piece of plastic — but in those days there was no plastic, it had not yet been discovered, it was a long time ago — I held it in my hand, a piece, like this, torn, with a small design which was very pretty. He told me how it had happened. When the medium had been put into trance, a person had appeared dressed in a robe of this substance — it was a materialisation; this person had passed in front of him and, like the little brute he was, he had torn off a piece to have a proof, and he kept the piece. The medium screamed — and everything, everything immediately vanished.... But the piece remained in his hand and he gave it to me. I gave it back to him. He had simply shown it to me, I held it in my hand.

So that was something quite concrete, you see, for he still had the piece; he could not tell himself it was a hallucination. Well, in spite of all this, in spite of the most extraordinary stories which could make a whole book, he did not believe *anything*! He could not explain *anything*. And he wondered who was mad, whether it was himself or the others or... This had not helped his knowledge progress even half a step forward. One cannot believe these things unless one carries them within oneself.

No external proofs you can have will ever give you any knowledge. When you *yourselves* are inwardly developed, are capable of having a direct and inner contact with these things, then you know what they are, but no material proof — material and of this kind — can give you the knowledge if within you you do not have the *being* capable of having this knowledge.

Therefore, the conclusion is that this kind of experiment is absolutely useless. For those who have an inner being, one day or another, life will see to it that they awaken and will bring them into contact with what they need in order to know.

I consider these things to be an unhealthy curiosity, that's all.

6 August 1958

> *Sweet Mother, what is the effect and value of collective prayer?*

We have already spoken about this, about collective prayers, the use that has been made of them. I believe that it has even been published in the *Bulletin*.

Besides, there are different kinds of collective prayer, just as there are different kinds of collectivities. There is the anonymous mass, the crowd, formed by chance circumstances, without any inner coordination, impelled by the force of circumstance, as for instance when a king or a person who attracts public attention is in a critical situation, either ill or the victim of an accident, and the people gather to obtain news and also to express their feelings; and through chance circumstances people have collected there, that is, there is no inner link except that of the same emotion or interest. There have been cases of crowds spontaneously beginning to pray to ask for the recovery of someone in whom they were specially interested. Of course, these very crowds can gather for a completely different purpose, out of hatred, and their cries are also a sort of prayer, a prayer to the adverse and destructive forces.

Those movements are spontaneous, not organised, unexpected.

There is also the collectivity formed by individuals who have gathered together around an ideal or a teaching or an action they want to carry out, and who have an organising link between them, the link of the same purpose, the same will and the same faith. These can gather in a methodical manner to practise common prayer and meditation, and if their aim is high, their organisation good, their ideal powerful, through their prayers or meditations these groups can have a considerable effect on world events or on their own inner development and collective progress. These groups are necessarily far superior to others, but they don't have the blind strength of the mobs, the collective action of the crowd. They replace this vehemence, this intensity by the strength of a deliberate and conscious organisation.

At all times there have been on earth groups organised in this way. Some of them have had a historical life, a historical action in the world, but as a rule they have not succeeded better with the crowd, the mass, than exceptional individuals. They have always been suspected and subjected to attacks, persecutions, and often they have also been dissolved in a very brutal, obscure and ignorant way.... There were those semi-religious, semi-chivalric groups, gathered around a belief or rather a creed, with a definite aim, which have had a very interesting history in the world. And certainly, they have done much for collective progress through their individual effort.

There is an ideal organisation which, if fully realised, could create a kind of very powerful unity, composed of elements all having the same aim and the same will and with enough inner development to be able to give a very coherent body to this inner oneness of purpose, motive, aspiration and action.

At all times centres of initiation have tried this, more or less successfully, and this is always mentioned in all occult traditions as an extremely powerful means of action.

If the collective unit could attain the same cohesion as the individual unit, it would multiply the strength and action of the individual.

Usually, if several individuals are brought together, the collective quality of the group is much lower than the individual value of each person taken separately, but with a sufficiently conscious and coordinated organisation, it would be possible, on the contrary, to *multiply* the power of individual action.

13 Agust 1958

Sweet Mother, in July 1953 you told us that after five years you would give us lessons on spiritual life.[1] I have brought what you said, Sweet Mother.

Really! That is interesting!
(*Mother reads the text given by the child*) Has it been printed?

No, Mother.

Oh! I like the last sentence very much!
(*After a silence*) So, what do you expect me to do?... To begin?

Yes, Mother.

But I have already started, haven't I? Even before the five years have passed! It seems that on that day, I... Oh! I wrote here — it is something I wrote...

It is written in Conversations,[2] Sweet Mother.

There I have written about the confusion made between asceticism and spiritual life, and then I promise that

1. See *Questions and Answers 1953* (15 July 1953).
2. Presently entitled *Questions and Answers 1929-1931*.

one day I shall speak to you about the confusion people make between what they call God and what I call the Divine.

But I have already spoken to you about that several times, haven't I?

I did not remember my promise but I have kept it without remembering it and even before the day came!

Now, if you ask me a precise question on this subject, I shall see what I can say. What do you want to know about spiritual life?... Do you have a particular question?

You mean you have started the meditations, Mother?

Yes!... And giving you explanations on what I read. We have even begun, in the small class, to meditate on the disciplines which are necessary to lead a spiritual life. And when I took up the reading of the Dhammapada, we read many things leading to the knowledge of spiritual life. But if you have a precise question on a special point, you can ask it, I shall reply.

Sweet Mother, why don't we profit as much as we should by our presence here in the Ashram?

Ah! That is very simple; it is because it is too easy!... When you have to go all round the world to find a teacher, when you have to give up everything to obtain only the first words of a teaching, then this teaching,

On "The Evolution of the Spiritual Man"

this spiritual help becomes something very precious, like everything that is difficult to obtain, and you make a great effort to deserve it.

Most of you came here when you were very small, at an age when there can be no question of the spiritual life or spiritual teaching — it would be altogether premature. You have indeed lived in this atmosphere but without even being aware of it; you are accustomed to seeing me, hearing me; I speak to you as one does to all children, I have even played with you as one plays with children; you only have to come and sit here and you hear me speak, you only have to ask me a question and I answer you, I have never refused to say anything to anybody — it is so easy. It is enough to... live — to sleep, to eat, to do exercises and study at school. You live here as you would live anywhere else. And so, you are used to it.

If I had made strict rules, if I had said, "I shall not tell you anything until you have truly made an effort to know it", then perhaps you might have made some effort, but that's not in keeping with my idea. I believe more in the power of the atmosphere and of example than of a rigorous teaching. I count more on something awakening in the being through contagion rather than by a methodical, disciplined effort.

Perhaps, after all, something is being prepared and one day it will spring up to the surface. That is what I hope for.

One day you will tell yourself, "Just think! I have been here so long, I could have learnt so much, realised so much and I never even thought of it! Only like that, now and then." And then, on that day... well, on that day, just imagine, you are going to wake up all of a sudden to something you never noticed but which is deep within you and thirsts for the truth, *thirsts* for transformation and is ready to make the effort required to realise it. On that day you will go very fast, you will advance with giant strides.... Perhaps, as I said, that day has come now after five years? I said, "I give you five years...." Now the five years have passed, so perhaps the day has come! Perhaps you will suddenly feel an *irresistible* need not to live in unconsciousness, in ignorance, in that state in which you do things without knowing why, feel things without understanding why, have contradictory wills, understand nothing about anything, live only by habit, routine, reactions — you take life easy. And one day you are no longer satisfied with that.

It depends, for each one it is different. Most often it is the need to know, to understand; for some it is the need to do what must be done as it should be done; for others it is a vague feeling that behind this life, so unconscious, so futile, so empty of meaning, there is something to find which is *worth* being lived — that there is a reality, a truth behind these falsehoods and illusions.

One suddenly feels that everything one does, everything one sees, has no meaning, no purpose, but that *there is* something which has a meaning; that essentially one is here on earth for something, that all this — all these movements, all this agitation, all this wastage of force and energy — all that must have a purpose, an aim, and that this uneasiness one feels within oneself,

On "The Evolution of the Spiritual Man"

this lack of satisfaction, this need, this *thirst* for something must lead us somewhere else.

And one day, you ask yourself, "But then, why is one born? Why does one die? Why does one suffer? Why does one act?"

You no longer live like a little machine, hardly half-conscious. You want to feel truly, to act truly, to know truly. Then, in ordinary life one searches for books, for people who know a little more than oneself, one begins to seek somebody who can solve these questions, lift the veil of ignorance. Here it is very simple. You only have to... do the things one does every day, but to do them with a purpose.

You go to the Samadhi, look at Sri Aurobindo's picture, you come to receive a flower from me, sit down to a lesson; you do everything you do but... with one question within you: Why?

And then, if you ask the question, you receive the answer. Why?

Because we don't want life as it is any longer, because we don't want falsehood and ignorance any longer, because we don't want suffering and unconsciousness any longer, because we do not want disorder and bad will any longer, because Sri Aurobindo has come to tell us: It is not necessary to leave the earth to find the Truth, it is not necessary to leave life to find one's soul, it is not necessary to give up the world or to have limited beliefs in order to enter into relation with the Divine. The Divine is everywhere, in everything, and if He is hidden... it is because we do not take the trouble to discover Him.

We can, simply by a sincere aspiration, open a sealed door in us and find... that Something which will change the whole significance of life, reply to all our questions, solve all our problems and lead us to the perfection we aspire for without knowing it, to that Reality which alone can satisfy us and give us lasting joy, equilibrium, strength, life.

All this you have heard many a time.

You have heard it — Oh! There are even some here who are so used to it that for them it seems to be the same thing as drinking a glass of water or opening a window to let in the sunlight.

But since I promised you that in five years you would be able *to live* these things, to have a concrete, real, convincing experience of them, well, that means you ought to be ready and that we are going to begin.

We have tried a little, but now we are going to try seriously!

The starting-point: to want it, truly want it, to need it. The next step: to think, *above all*, of that. A day comes, very quickly, when one is unable to think of anything else.

That is the one thing which counts. And then...

One formulates one's aspiration, lets the true prayer spring up from one's heart, the prayer which expresses the sincerity of the need. And then... well, one will see what happens.

Something will happen. Surely something will happen. For each one it will take a different form.

That's all. I am glad you gave me this.

15 August 1958

This short talk was given on a Friday,
the day on which the Dhammapada was
usually read.

As today is Sri Aurobindo's birthday I thought that instead of reading the Dhammapada I could read to you something which will both interest you and show you how Sri Aurobindo visualised our relation with the gods.

You know, don't you, that in India especially, there are countless categories of gods, who are all on different planes, some very close to man, others very close to the Supreme, with many intermediaries.

You will understand better what I want to tell you if I mention the gods of the Puranas — like those we saw the other day in the film — who in many ways are, I must say, inferior to man (!) although they have infinitely more power.

There are gods of the Overmind who are the great creators of the earth — until now. There are the gods of the Vedas who are mentioned in everything that has come down from the Rishis. And there are the gods of the Supermind, those who are going to manifest on earth, although of course they exist from all eternity on their own plane.

Here Sri Aurobindo is speaking mostly about the Vedic gods, but not exclusively nor in a very definite way. At any rate these gods are higher than the gods of the Puranas.

Here is what Sri Aurobindo tells us.

In fact, it is a prayer:

> Be wide in me, O Varuna;
> be mighty in me, O Indra;
> O Sun, be very bright and luminous;
> O Moon, be full of charm and sweetness.
> Be fierce and terrible, O Rudra;
> be impetuous and swift, O Maruts;
> be strong and bold, O Aryama;
> be voluptuous and pleasurable, O Bhaga;
> be tender and kind and loving and passionate, O Mitra.
> Be bright and revealing, O Dawn;
> O Night, be solemn and pregnant.
> O Life, be full, ready and buoyant;
> O Death, lead my steps from mansion to mansion.
> Harmonise all these, O Brahmanaspati.
> Let me not be subject to these gods, O Kali.[1]

So Sri Aurobindo makes Kali the great liberating power who ardently impels you towards progress and leaves no ties within you which would hinder you from progressing.

I think this will be a good subject for meditation.

(Meditation)

---

1. *Thoughts and Aphorisms,* SABCL, Vol. 17, p. 85.

27 August 1958

Sweet Mother, when you tell us to meditate on a subject, we choose, for instance, to meditate that we are opening to the light; we imagine all sorts of strange things, we imagine a door opening, etc., but this always takes a mental form.

It depends on the individual. Everyone has his own particular process. It depends altogether on each one. Some people may have an imagery which helps them; others, on the contrary, have a more abstract mind and only see ideas; others, who live more in sensations or feelings, have rather psychological movements, movements of inner feelings or sensations — it depends on each one. Those who have an active and particularly formative physical mind, see images, but everybody does not experience the same thing. If you ask the person next to you, for instance... (*To the next child*) When I give a subject, do you see images like that?

Sometimes.

Sometimes?

Most often I feel something.

What is it, most often?

A sensation.

A sensation, yes. It is more frequently a sensation — I mean generally — more frequently a sensation or a feeling than an image. The image always comes to those who have a formative mental power, an active physical mind. It is an indication that one is active in one's mental consciousness.

(The child who had asked the first question) *But is this right?*

But everything is right if it has a result! Any means is good. Why shouldn't it be right?... Images like that are not necessarily ridiculous. They are not ridiculous, they are mental images. If they bring you some result, they are quite appropriate. If they give you an experience, they are appropriate.

For example, when I ask you to go deep down within yourselves, some of you will concentrate on a sensation, but others may just as well have the impression of going down into a deep well, and they clearly see the picture of steps going down into a dark and deep well, and they go down farther and farther, deeper and deeper, and sometimes reach precisely a door; they sit down before the door with the will to enter, and sometimes the door opens, and then they go in and see a kind of hall or a room or a cave or something, and from there, if they go on they may come to another door and again stop, and with an effort the door opens and they go farther.

On "The Evolution of the Spiritual Man"   217

And if this is done with enough persistence and one can continue the experience, there comes a time when one finds oneself in front of a door which has... a special kind of solidity or solemnity, and with a great effort of concentration the door opens and one suddenly enters a hall of clarity, of light; and then, one has the experience, you see, of contact with one's soul.... But I don't see what is bad in having images!

No, but it is only an imagination, isn't it, Mother?

An imagination? But what is an imagination?... You cannot imagine anything which doesn't exist in the universe! It is impossible to imagine something that doesn't exist somewhere. The only possibility is that one may not put one's image in its place: either one gives it virtues and qualities it doesn't have, or explains it with some other than the right explanation. But whatever one imagines exists somewhere; the main thing is to know where and to put it in its proper place.

Of course, if after having imagined that you are in front of a door which is opening, you thought that it was really a physical door inside your body, that would be a mistake! But if you realise that it is the mental form taken by your effort of concentration, this is quite correct. If you go wandering in the mental world, you will see plenty of forms like that, all kinds of forms, which have no material reality but truly exist in the mental world.

You cannot think powerfully of something without

your thought taking a form. But if you were to believe that this form was physical, that would obviously be an error, yet it really does exist in the mental world.

Imagination is a power of formation. In fact, people who have no imagination are not formative from the mental point of view, they cannot give a concrete power to their thought. Imagination is a very powerful means of action. For instance, if you have a pain somewhere and if you imagine that you are making the pain disappear or are removing it or destroying it — all kinds of images like that — well, you succeed perfectly.

There's a story of a person who was losing her hair at a fantastic rate, enough to become bald within a few weeks, and then someone told her, "When you brush your hair, imagine that it is growing and will grow very fast." And always, while brushing her hair, she said, "Oh, my hair is growing! Oh, it will grow very fast!..." — And it happened! But what people usually do is to tell themselves, "Ah, all my hair is falling again and I shall become bald, that's certain, it's going to happen!"

And of course it happens!

Mother, in the Friday Classes, you often read a sentence[1] to us and ask us to meditate on it. But how should we meditate on a sentence? That is, should we think, meditate on the idea or... what should we do?

---

1. At that time it was from the Dhammapada.

On "The Evolution of the Spiritual Man"

Meditate on a sentence?

Yes.

Obviously on what it means.

That is, we must think...

Yes. Then?

Because that, Mother, becomes a mental function or what?

The sentence is already a mental formation; the mental formation is made. The sentence is the expression of the mental formation. So when you meditate on a sentence, there are two methods. There is an active, ordinary external method of reflecting and trying to understand what these words mean, understand intellectually what the sentence means exactly — that is active meditation. You concentrate on these few words and take the thought they express and try, through reasoning, deduction, analysis, to understand what it means.

There is another method, more direct and deep; it is to take this mental formation, this combination of words with the thought they represent, and to gather all your energy of attention on it, compelling yourself to concentrate all your strength on that formation. For instance, instead of concentrating all your energies on something you see physically, you take that thought and concentrate all your energies on that thought — in the mind, of course.

And then, if you are able to concentrate the thought sufficiently and stop it from vacillating, you pass quite naturally from the thought expressed by the words to the *idea* which is behind and which could be expressed in other words, other forms. The characteristic of the idea is the power to clothe itself in many different thoughts. And when you have achieved this, you have already gone much deeper than by merely understanding the words. Naturally, if you continue to concentrate and know how to do it, you can pass from the idea to the luminous force that is behind. Then you enter a much vaster and deeper domain. But that asks for some training. But still, that is the very principle of meditation.

If you are able to go deep enough, you find the Principle and the Force behind the idea, and that gives you the power of realisation. This is how those who take meditation as a means of spiritual development are able to unite with the Principle which is behind things and obtain the power to act on these things from above.

But even without going so far — that implies a rather hard discipline, doesn't it, a long-standing habit — you can pass quite easily from the thought to the idea, and that gives you a light and an understanding in the mind which enables you, in your turn, to express the idea in any form. An idea can be expressed in many different forms, in many different thoughts, just as when you come down to a more material level, a thought can be expressed through many different words. Going

On "The Evolution of the Spiritual Man"

downwards, towards expression, that is, spoken or written expression, there are many different words and different formulas which may serve to express a thought, but this thought is only one of the forms of thought which can express the idea, the idea behind, and this idea itself, if it is followed deeply, has behind it a principle of spiritual knowledge and power which can then spread and act on the manifestation.

When you have a thought you look for words, don't you, and then you try to arrange these words to express your thought; you can use many words to express a thought, you tell yourself, "No, look, if I put this word instead of that, it would express what I am thinking much better." That is what you learn when you are taught style, how to write.

But when I give you a written sentence which has the power to express a thought and tell you to concentrate on it, then, through this thought-form you can go back to the idea behind, which can be expressed in many different thoughts. It is like a great hierarchy: there is a Principle right at the top, which itself is not the only one, for you can go still higher up; but this Principle can be expressed in ideas, and these ideas can be expressed in a great number of thoughts and this great number of thoughts can make use of many languages and an even greater number of words.

When I give you a thought it is simply to help you to concentrate.... There are schools which put an object in front of you, a flower or a stone, or any object, and then you sit around it and concentrate on it and your eyes go like this (*Mother squints*) until you become the object. That too is a method of concentration. By gazing steadily like that, without moving, you finally pass into the thing you are gazing at. But you must not begin to gaze at all kinds of things: only gaze steadily at that. That gives you a look... it makes you squint.

All this is to learn concentration, that's all. Sometimes one of these sentences expresses a very deep truth. It is one of those happy sentences which are very expressive. So that helps you to find the truth that is behind.

When we have finished the Dhammapada, that is what I intend to do. I am at present translating the latest of Sri Aurobindo's books we have published, *Thoughts and Aphorisms*, and I intend, every Friday, to give one single sentence, one single aphorism — with or without the commentary as necessary — as a subject for meditation. We still have to see how we should go about it.... We could proceed in two different ways. As I am going to take them up in order, you will always know which one will be for the following week and prepare questions in advance; or else if you don't prepare the questions in advance, perhaps it will be more interesting to take a sentence, to have a meditation on it, and in the following lesson to ask me questions on the sentence from the previous week. Then, from the questions I am asked, I shall choose those that seem to me the most intelligent and answer them. And later we shall take a new sentence which will serve as the subject for meditation on that day and the subject for questions the following week. And this I am going to do with a very precise, very definite purpose: to bring you out of your mental somnolence and compel you to reflect and try to understand what I tell you.... For, it makes a little noise in your ears, a still softer noise in your heads, and then it goes out from the other side, and then it is finished! Sometimes, very rarely, by a special grace, there is just a little effect here, like this (*gesture*), which lasts like a little flickering flame — it burns, and then, pfft!... Something blows on it, it goes out and it is all finished.

We need lessons, Sweet Mother.

When you told me the other day that I had promised to give you "lessons", well, I took it very seriously. I am going to keep my promise. There.

3 September 1958

Sweet Mother, the other day you told me that it was necessary to learn how to discipline the imagination.

Yes.

How is it done?

Imagination is something very complex and manifold — what is vaguely called "imagination".

It can be the capacity for seeing and recording, noting the forms in some mental or other domain. There are artistic, literary, poetic domains, domains of action, scientific domains, all belonging to the mind — not a very high and abstract mind, a mind above the physical mind which, without our knowing it, pours out constantly through the individual and collective mind to manifest in action.

Some people, through a special faculty, are in contact with these domains, take up one formation or other that is there, draw them to themselves and give them an expression. This power of expression is different in different people, but those who can open themselves to these domains, to see things there, to draw these forms towards themselves and express them — either in literature or in painting or music or in action or science — are, according to the degree of their power of expression

On "The Evolution of the Spiritual Man" 225

either very highly talented beings or else geniuses.

There are higher geniuses still. They are people who can open to a higher region, a higher force which, passing through the mental layers, comes and takes a form in a human mind and reveals itself in the world as new truths, new philosophical systems, new spiritual teachings, which are the works and at the same time the actions of the great beings who come to take birth on earth. That is an imagination which can be called "Truth-imagination".

These higher forces, when they come down into the earth-atmosphere, take living, active, powerful forms, spread throughout the world and prepare a new age.

These two kinds of imagination are what could be called higher imaginations.

And now, to come down to a more ordinary level, everyone has in him, in a greater or lesser measure, the power to give form to his mental activity and use this form either in his ordinary activity or to create and realise something. We are all the time, always, creating images, creating forms. We send them into the atmosphere without even knowing that we are doing so — they go roaming about, pass from one person to another, meet companions, sometimes join together and get on happily, sometimes create conflicts, and there are battles; for often, very often, in these mental imaginations there is a small element of will which tries to realise itself, and then everyone tries to send out his formation so that it can act, so that things can happen as he wants and, as everyone does this, it creates a general confusion. If our eyes were open to the vision of all these forms in the atmosphere, we would see very amazing things: battlefields, waves, onsets, retreats of a *crowd* of small mental entities which are constantly thrown out into the air and always try to realise themselves. All these formations have a common tendency to want to materialise and realise themselves physically, and as they are countless — they are far too many for there to be room enough on earth to manifest them — they jostle and elbow one another, they try to push back those which do not agree with them or even form armies marching in good order, always to take up the available room both in time and space — it is only a very small space compared with the countless number of creations.

So, individually, this is what happens. Some people do all that without knowing it — perhaps everybody — and they are constantly tossed from one thing to another, and hope, wish, desire, are disappointed, sometimes happy, sometimes in despair, for they don't have any control or mastery over these things. But the beginning of wisdom is to look at ourselves thinking and to see this phenomenon, become aware of this constant projection into the atmosphere of small *living* entities which are trying to manifest. All this comes out of the mental atmosphere which we carry within ourselves. Once we see and observe, we can begin to sort them out, that is, to push back what is not in conformity with our highest will or aspiration and allow to move towards manifestation only the formations which can help us to progress and develop normally.

This is the control of active thought, and that was what I meant the other day.

How many times you sit and become aware that the thought is beginning to form images for itself, to tell itself a story; and so, when you have become a little expert at it, not only do you see unfolding before you the history of what you would like to happen in life, in your own life, but you can take something away, add a detail, perfect your work, make a really *fine* story in which everything conforms with your highest aspiration. And once you have made a complete harmonious construction, as perfect as you can make it, then you open your hands and let the bird fly away.

If it is well made, it always realises itself in the end. And that is what one doesn't know.

But the thing is realised in the course of time, sometimes long afterwards, when you have forgotten your story, can no longer remember having told it to yourself — you have changed much, are thinking about other things, making other stories, and the first one no longer interests you; and if you are not very attentive, when the result of the first story comes, you are already very far away from it and no longer remember at all that this is the result of your own story.... And that is why it is so important to control yourself, for if within you there are multiple and contradictory wills — not only wills but tendencies, orientations, levels of life — all this causes battles in your life. For example, at your highest level you have fashioned a beautiful story which you send out into the world, but then, perhaps the next day, perhaps on the very same day, perhaps a little later, you have come down to a much more material level, and these things from above seem to you a little... fairylike, unreal; and you begin to make very concrete, very utilitarian formations which are not always very pretty... and these too go out.

I have known people with such opposite sides in their nature, so contradictory, that one day they could make a magnificent, luminous, powerful formation for realisation, and then the next day a defeatist, dark, black formation — a formation of despair — and so both would go out. And I was able to follow in the course of circumstances the beautiful one being realised, and while it was being realised, the dark one demolishing what the first one had done. And that is how it is in the larger lines of life as in its smaller details. And all that because one does not watch oneself thinking, because one believes one is the slave of these contradictory movements, because one says, "Oh! Today I am not feeling well. Oh! Today things seem sad to me", and one says this as if it were an ineluctable fate against which one could do nothing. But if one stands back or ascends a step, one can look at all these things, put them in their place, keep some, destroy or get rid of those one does not want and put all one's imaginative power — what is called imaginative — only in those one wants and which conform with one's highest aspiration. That is what I call controlling one's imagination.

It is very interesting. When one learns to do it and does it regularly one no longer has time to feel bored.

And instead of being a cork afloat on the waves of the sea and tossed here and there by each wave, defencelessly, one becomes a bird which opens its wings, flies above the waves and goes wherever it wants. That's all.

10 September 1958

"In modern times, as physical Science enlarged its discoveries and released the secret material forces of Nature into an action governed by human knowledge for human use, occultism receded and was finally set aside on the ground that the physical alone is real and Mind and Life are only departmental activities of Matter. On this basis, believing material Energy to be the key of all things, Science has attempted to move towards a control of mind and life processes by a knowledge of the material instrumentation and process of our normal and abnormal mind and life functionings and activities; the spiritual is ignored as only one form of mentality. It may be observed in passing that if this endeavour succeeded, it might not be without danger for the existence of the human race, even as now are certain other scientific discoveries misused or clumsily used by a humanity mentally and morally unready for the handling of powers so great and perilous; for it would be an artificial control applied without any knowledge of the secret forces which underlie and sustain our existence. Occultism in the West could be thus easily pushed aside because it never reached its majority, never acquired ripeness and a philosophic or sound systematic foundation. It indulged too freely in the romance of the supernatural or made the mistake of concentrating its major effort on the discovery

of formulas and effective modes for using supernormal powers. It deviated into magic white and black or into a romantic or thaumaturgic paraphernalia of occult mysticism and the exaggeration of what was after all a limited and scanty knowledge. These tendencies and this insecurity of mental foundation made it difficult to defend and easy to discredit, a target facile and vulnerable. In Egypt and the East this line of knowledge arrived at a greater and more comprehensive endeavour: this ampler maturity can be seen still intact in the remarkable system of the Tantras; it was not only a many-sided science of the supernormal but supplied the basis of all the occult elements of religion and even developed a great and powerful system of spiritual discipline and self-realisation. For the highest occultism is that which discovers the secret movements and dynamic supernormal possibilities of Mind and Life and Spirit and uses them in their native force or by an applied process for the greater effectivity of our mental, vital and spiritual being. "Occultism is associated in popular idea with magic and magical formulas and a supposed mechanism of the supernatural. But this is only one side, nor is it altogether a superstition as is vainly imagined by those who have not looked deeply or at all at this covert side of secret Nature-Force or experimented with its possibilities. Formulas and their application, a mechanisation of latent forces, can be astonishingly effective in the occult use of mind-power and life-power just as it is in physical Science, but this is only a subordinate method and a limited direction. For mind and life forces are plastic, subtle and variable in their action and have not the material rigidity; they need a subtle and plastic intuition in the knowledge of them, in the interpretation of their action and process and in their application, — even in the interpretation and action of their established formulas. An overstress on mechanisation and rigid formulation is likely to result in sterilisation or a formalised limitation of knowledge and, on the pragmatic side, to much error, ignorant convention, misuse and failure. Now that we are outgrowing the superstition of the sole truth of Matter, a swing backward towards the old occultism and to new formulations, as well as to a scientific investigation of the still hidden secrets and powers of Mind and a close study of psychic and abnormal or supernormal psychological phenomena, is possible and, in parts, already visible. But if it is to fulfil itself, the true foundation, the true aim and direction, the necessary restrictions and precautions of this line of inquiry have to be rediscovered; its most important aim must be the discovery of the hidden truths and powers of the mind-force and the life-power and the greater forces of the concealed spirit. Occult science is, essentially, the science of the subliminal, the subliminal in ourselves and the subliminal in world-nature, and of all that is in connection with the subliminal, including the subconscient and the superconscient, and the use of it as

part of self-knowledge and world-knowledge and for the right dynamisation of that knowledge."
The Life Divine, SABCL, Vol. 19, pp. 875-77

Sweet Mother, what is white magic?

What we call "white magic" is a beneficial magic and "black magic" is a harmful magic. But in fact these are mere words, they have no meaning.

Magic?... It is a knowledge that has been reduced to purely material formulas. They are some kind of words or numbers or combinations of words and numbers, which, if they are simply pronounced or written, even by someone who has no inner power, must act. In occultism, this is what corresponds to chemical formulas in science. You see, in science you have chemical formulas for combining certain elements and producing others from them; even if you do not have any mental or vital or even physical power, if you just follow to the letter the formula you have, you obtain the required result — it is enough simply to have a memory. Well, the same thing has been tried in occultism, making combinations of sounds, letters, numbers, words, which, by their inherent qualities, have the power to obtain a certain result. In this way, any fool, if he learns this and does exactly what he is told, obtains — or believes he will obtain — the result he wants. While... let us take the mantra, for instance, which is a form of occultism; unless the mantra is given by a guru and the guru transmits his occult or spiritual power to you with the mantra, you may repeat your mantra thousands of times, it will have no effect.

That is to say, in true occultism, one must have the quality, the ability, the inner gift in order to use it, and that is the safeguard. True occultism cannot be practised by any fool. And this is no longer magic — neither white magic nor black nor golden — it is not magic at all, it is a spiritual power which must be acquired by long discipline; and finally, it is given to you only by a divine grace.

This means that as soon as one draws near the Truth, one is safe from all charlatanism, all pretension and falsehood. Of this I have had numerous and extremely conclusive proofs. And so someone who has the true occult power possesses at the same time, by the strength of this inner truth, the power to undo any magic, white or black or whatever colour it may be, simply by applying a drop of that truth, one might say. There is nothing that can resist that power. And this is very well known to those who practise magic, for they always take very great care, in all countries but especially in India, never to try out any of their formulas against yogis and saints, because they know that these formulas which they send out with their little mechanical, very superficial power, will go and strike, like a ball on a wall, the true power that protects one who leads a spiritual life, and quite naturally their formula will rebound and fall back on them.

The yogi or saint doesn't need to do anything, he doesn't even have to want to protect himself: it is something automatic. He is in a state of consciousness and

On "The Evolution of the Spiritual Man" 235

inner power which automatically protects him from everything that is inferior. Naturally, he can also use his power deliberately to protect others. This rebounding of the bad formation from his atmosphere automatically protects him, but if this bad formation is made against someone he is protecting or simply someone who asks for his help, then he can, by a movement of his own atmosphere, his own aura, surround the person who is exposed to the evil magic spells, and the rebounding process acts in the same way and causes the bad formation to fall back quite naturally on the one who made it. But in this case the conscious will of the yogi or saint or sage is needed. He has to be informed about what has happened and he must decide to intervene.

That is the difference between true knowledge and magic.

Anything else?... Is that all?

Mother, can physical science by its progress open to occultism?

It does not call it "occultism", that's all. It is only a question of words.... They are making sensational discoveries which people with occult knowledge already knew thousands of years ago! They have made a long circuit and come to the same thing.

With the most recent discoveries in medicine, in the applied sciences, for instance, they are contacting in this way, with a wonder-struck interest, things which were known to certain sages a very, very long time ago. And then they present all this before you as new marvels — but indeed they are rather old, their marvels!

They will end up by practising occultism without knowing that they are doing so! For, in fact, as soon as one draws close, however slightly, to the truth of things and when one is sincere in one's search, not satisfied by mere appearances, when one really wants to find something and goes deep, penetrates behind appearances, then one begins to advance towards the truth of things; and as one comes closer to it, well, one finds again the same knowledge that others who began by going within have brought back from their inner discoveries.

Only the method and the path are different but the thing discovered will be the same, because there are not two things to be found, there is only one. It will necessarily be the same. It all depends on the path one follows; some go fast, others slowly, some go straight, others, as I said, go a long way round — and what labour! How they have laboured!... Besides, it is very respectable.

(Silence)

Now they are finding out that they can replace anaesthetics by hypnotism with infinitely better results. Well, hypnotism is a form — a form modernised in its expression — of occultism; a very limited, very small form of a very tiny power compared with occult power, but still it is a form of occultism which has been put in modern terms to make the thing modern. And I don't know if you have heard about these things, but they are very interesting from a certain point of view: for instance, this process of hypnotism has been tried on someone who had to have a skin graft on a wound. I don't remember all the details now, but the arm had to remain attached to the leg for a fortnight.... If the person were immobilised by plaster and bandages and all sorts of things, at the end of the fortnight he wouldn't be able to move — everything would become stiff and he would need weeks of treatment to recover the free use of his arm. In this case, nothing was tied up, nothing was physically immobilised — no plaster, no bandages, nothing — the person was just hypnotised and told to keep his arm in that position. He kept it for a fortnight, without any effort, any difficulty, without any intervention from his will: it was the will of the hypnotiser which intervened. It was perfectly successful, the arm remained in the required position, and when the fortnight was over and the hypnotism removed, and the person was told, "Now you may move", he began to move! Well, that's a step forward.

They are soon going to meet — it will be nothing more than a question of words — then, if they are not too rigid, they can agree on the value given to the words!

Sweet Mother, they say hypnotism has a bad after-effect on the hypnotised person?

No, no! If somebody practises hypnotism to impose his will on another, it can obviously do much harm to the other person, but we are speaking of a hypnotism which is practised in a humanitarian way, it might be said, and for precise reasons.

All the bad effects can be avoided if the one who does it has no bad intentions.

If you use chemical formulas in an ignorant way, you can cause an explosion (*laughter*), and that is very dangerous! Well, if you use occult formulas ignorantly — or egoistically, which is even worse than ignorantly — you can also have harmful results. But that doesn't mean that occultism is bad or hypnotism is bad or chemistry is bad. You are not going to ban chemistry because there are people who cause explosions! (*Laughter*)

To learn occultism one must have special qualities, whereas for learning science...

But for everything one must have special qualities!

Scientific knowledge is accessible to all.

Listen, if you are not an artist, you may work for years with paint-brushes, colours, canvases, and spend much money and much effort, and yet produce horrible things. If you are not a musician, you may labour hard for hours at playing the piano and you will never do anything worthwhile. Special qualities are always needed.... Why, even for an athlete — if you are not born an athlete, you may try as hard as you like, you will only succeed in doing something quite mediocre and

On "The Evolution of the Spiritual Man" 239

ordinary. It will be better than someone who does not try at all, but that does not mean that you are automatically going to succeed. Besides, if we go a step further, everyone has countless possibilities within him of which he is unaware and which develop only if he does what is to be done in the way it should be done.... But there are two types of progress, not only one; there is the progress that consists in perfecting more and more the capacities, possibilities, faculties and qualities you have — this is what is normally obtained by education; but if you go in for a little more thorough development by approaching a deeper truth, you can add, to the qualities you already have, other new ones which seem to be asleep in your being.

You can multiply your possibilities, enlarge and increase them; you can suddenly bring up something you did not think you had. I have already explained this to you several times. When one discovers one's psychic being within, at the same time there develop and manifest, quite unexpectedly, things one could not do at all before and which one didn't think were in one's nature. Of this too I have had numerous examples. I have given you this one, but I am repeating it to you once more to make myself understood.

I used to know a young girl who was born in a very ordinary environment, who had not received much education and wrote rather clumsy French, who had not developed her imagination and had absolutely no literary sense: that seemed to be among the possibilities she did not have. Well, when she had the inner experience of contact with her psychic being, and as long as the contact was living and very present, she wrote admirable things. When she fell back from that state into an ordinary one, she could not even put two sentences together correctly! And I saw examples of both kinds of her writing.

There is a genius within everyone of us — we don't know it. We must find the way to make it come out — but it is there sleeping, it asks for nothing better than to manifest; we must open the door to it.

17 September 1958

"An intellectual approach to the highest knowledge, the mind's possession of it, is an indispensable aid to this movement of Nature in the human being. Ordinarily, on our surface, man's chief instrument of thought and action is the reason, the observing, understanding and arranging intellect. In any total advance or evolution of the Spirit, not only the intuition, insight, inner sense, the heart's devotion, a deep and direct life-experience of the things of the Spirit have to be developed, but the intellect also must be enlightened and satisfied; our thinking and reflecting mind must be helped to understand, to form a reasoned and systematised idea of the goal, the method, the principles of this highest development and activity of our nature and the truth of all that lies behind it. Spiritual realisation and experience, an intuitive and direct knowledge, a growth of inner consciousness, a growth of the soul and of an intimate soul-perception, soul-vision and a soul-sense, are indeed the proper means of this evolution: but the support of the reflective and critical reason is also of great importance; if many can dispense with it, because they have a vivid and direct contact with inner realities and are satisfied with experience and insight, yet in the whole movement it is indispensable. If the supreme truth is a spiritual Reality, then the intellect of man needs to know what is the

> *nature of that original Truth and the principle of its relations to the rest of existence, to ourselves and the universe. The intellect is not capable by itself of bringing us into touch with the concrete spiritual reality, but it can help by a mental formulation of the truth of the Spirit which explains it to the mind and can be applied even in the more direct seeking: this help is of a capital importance."*
>
> The Life Divine, SABCL, Vol. 19, pp. 877-78

Sweet Mother, here Sri Aurobindo writes: "An intellectual approach to the highest knowledge, the mind's possession of it..." How is this possible?

Everything that happens to us in the spiritual world we always have a tendency to translate mentally; we want to explain it to ourselves, draw conclusions from it, change the experience into a rule of action, profit mentally by what has happened in order to transform the experience into something practically useful. That is what Sri Aurobindo calls "the mind's possession of it". This is done automatically, so to say. Unfortunately, the best part of the experience always escapes; and besides, if one wants to keep it intact, one would have to remain in a state in which the experience is not mentalised, and if one lives in the outer world this is practically impossible. That is why those who wished to enjoy their spiritual experience without intervention from the mind used to remain in states of trance and to carefully avoid coming down to the level of action. But if one wants to

On "The Evolution of the Spiritual Man" 243

transform life, if one wants the spiritual experience to have an effect on the mind, the vital and the body, on the daily activities, it is indispensable to try to express it mentally and accept the inevitable diminution, until the mind itself is transformed and capable of participating in the experience without deforming it.

What we want to do is still more difficult, for we want the vital also to be transformed and capable of participating in the experience without deforming it, and finally the physical itself, the body, to be transformed by the spiritual action and no longer be an obstacle to the experience.

This transformation is precisely the point that ordinary thought finds most difficult to accept, for it is almost the faculty of thought itself which must be changed. Its whole functioning has to be changed for this transformation to be possible, and we are so used to identifying the faculty with its functioning that we wonder if it is possible to think otherwise than in the way we ordinarily do.

It is possible only when one has had the experience of complete silence in the mental region and when the spiritual force with its light and power descends through the mind and makes it act directly without its following its usual method of analysis, deduction, reasoning. All these faculties which are usually considered the normal activities of the mind, must be stopped, and yet the spiritual Light, Knowledge and Power must be able to transform them into a channel of direct expression, without using these means to express themselves.

The mind, in its outermost form, is a means of action, an instrument for organisation and execution. It puts concepts in order, relates them to one another, draws conclusions for action from them and gives impulse to this action. This power of organisation and impulse to action can be produced directly by the spiritual force which takes hold of the mental consciousness without these processes of analysis, deduction, reasoning being necessary. In intuition things already happen somewhat in this way; but spiritual intervention is, as it were, a super-intuition, a direct expression of the vision, of the experience, of knowledge by identity.

(*Silence*)

There are many stages in this transformation and the first are like a kind of mental imitation of the movement. The whole process of analysis, reasoning, deduction and formulation of conclusions occurs almost spontaneously in a mental background and gives us the result which seems to us an intuition but which is still the result of all that work which was carried out very swiftly and, as I said, in a sort of background of which we are not fully conscious, so that we see the starting-point and the result without following the whole process in detail, the whole development of the mental activity. People who have a very quick mind and can grasp things very fast, people whose mental activity is extremely swift, immediate, can give the impression that they have intuition but this is only an outer form and almost an imitation

On "The Evolution of the Spiritual Man" 245

of true intuition. Intuition is already a direct vision, something that dispenses with reasoning and deduction. Through intuition there is already an expression of direct knowledge.

But before reaching this stage, all the experiences one has must pass through the ordinary mental method of observation, analysis and deduction in order to reach the outer consciousness. The very essence of the experience fades away and there remains only a sort of very dry husk which has lost all its power of realisation — almost, almost lost it.

But those whose intellectual activity is very dominant find it almost absolutely necessary to catch hold of everything, all inner experiences, and to begin to formulate them. If, in addition, they have a power of expression, they try to formulate them in words and sentences; and when one has lived these experiences and becomes aware of the descending curve, one sees at each stage the deep reality of the experience withdrawing, fading into the background, instead of being in the forefront and commanding the whole being; it retreats slowly like this (*gesture*), and outside there remains only something... which is a kind of dry and cold imitation. It may be expressed in very enthusiastic words, but in comparison with what the thing itself was, in itself, in its deep truth, it is so shrivelled up, diminished.... All the true joy, the true beauty, the inner enthusiasm, that wonderful warmth of the experience — all this retreats far behind. You try to keep a hold on it, but it eludes you. And you pay dearly for this power of formulation.

Mother, in our life here, what do we mean by the "development of the mind"? And how is it useful?

I believe I have already explained this to you once. I think I have even explained it in detail in the articles on education. It is quite similar to the results of physical education for the body.

We have limbs and muscles and nerves, indeed everything that constitutes the body; if we don't give them a special development, a special education, all these things do what they can to express the Power in the body, but it is a very clumsy and very incomplete expression. It is beyond question that a physical body which has been trained according to the most complete and rational methods of physical culture is capable of things it could never do otherwise. I think no one can deny that. Well, for the mind it is the same thing. You have a mental instrument with many possibilities, faculties, but they are latent and need a special education, a special training so that they can express the Light. It is certain that in ordinary life the brain is the seat of the outer expression of the mental consciousness; well, if this brain is not developed, if it is crude, there are innumerable things which cannot be expressed, because they do not have the instrument required to express themselves. It would be like a musical instrument with most of its notes missing, and that produces a rough approximation but not something precise.

Mental culture, intellectual education changes the constitution of your brain, enlarges it considerably, and

On "The Evolution of the Spiritual Man"

as a result the expression becomes more complete and more precise.

It is not necessary if you want to escape from life and go into inexpressible heights, but it is indispensable if you want to express your experience in outer life.

Mother, you said that if one develops these faculties of analysis, deduction and all that too much, they become obstacles to spiritual experiences, no?

If they are not controlled, mastered, yes. But not necessarily. Not necessarily. It might make the control a little more difficult, for naturally it is more difficult to master an individualised being than a crude one — with a completer individualisation the ego becomes more crystallised and also self-satisfied, doesn't it?... But granting that this difficulty has been overcome, well, in a highly developed individuality the result is infinitely superior to the one obtained in a crude and uneducated nature. I am not saying that the process of transformation or rather of consecration is not more difficult but once it is achieved the result is far superior.

This may very well be compared with musical instruments, one of which has a certain number of notes and the other ten times as many. Well, it is perhaps easier to play an instrument of four or five notes but the music that could be played on a complete keyboard is obviously far superior!

One could even compare this to an orchestra much more than to a simple instrument. A human being, a fully developed human individuality is very much like one of those stupendous orchestras which has hundreds and hundreds of players. It is obviously very difficult to control and conduct them but the result can be marvellous.

24 September 1958

"Our thinking mind is concerned mainly with the statement of general spiritual truth, the logic of its absolute and the logic of its relativities, how they stand to each other or lead to each other, and what are the mental consequences of the spiritual theorem of existence....

"The means by which this need [of intellectual understanding] can be satisfied and with which our nature of mind has provided us is philosophy, and in this field it must be a spiritual philosophy. Such systems have arisen in numbers in the East; for almost always, wherever there has been a considerable spiritual development, there has arisen from it a philosophy justifying it to the intellect. The method was at first an intuitive seeing and an intuitive expression, as in the fathomless thought and profound language of the Upanishads, but afterwards there was developed a critical method, a firm system of dialectics, a logical organisation. The later philosophies were an intellectual account[1] or a logical justification of what had been found by inner realisation; or they provided themselves with a mental ground or a systematised method for realisation and experience.[2] In the West where the syncretic tendency of

1. E.g., the Gita.
2. E.g., the Yoga philosophy of Patanjali.

the consciousness was replaced by the analytic and separative, the spiritual urge and the intellectual reason parted company almost at the outset; philosophy took from the first a turn towards a purely intellectual and ratiocinative explanation of things. Nevertheless, there were systems like the Pythagorean, Stoic, and Epicurean, which were dynamic not only for thought but for conduct of life and developed a discipline, an effort at inner perfection of the being; this reached a higher spiritual plane of knowledge in later Christian or Neo-pagan thought-structures where East and West met together. But later on the intellectualisation became complete and the connection of philosophy with life and its energies or spirit and its dynamism was either cut or confined to the little that the metaphysical idea can impress on life and action by an abstract and secondary influence. Religion has supported itself in the West not by philosophy but by a credal theology; sometimes a spiritual philosophy emerges by sheer force of individual genius, but it has not been as in the East a necessary adjunct to every considerable line of spiritual experience and endeavour. It is true that a philosophic development of spiritual thought is not entirely indispensable; for the truths of spirit can be reached more directly and completely by intuition and by a concrete inner contact. It must also be said that the critical control of the intellect over spiritual experience can be hampering and unreliable, for it is an inferior light turned upon a field of higher

illumination; the true controlling power is an inner discrimination, a psychic sense and tact, a superior intervention of guidance from above or an innate and luminous inner guidance. But still this line of development too is necessary, because there must be a bridge between the spirit and the intellectual reason: the light of a spiritual or at least a spiritualised intelligence is necessary for the fullness of our total inner evolution, and without it, if another deeper guidance is lacking, the inner movement may be erratic and undisciplined, turbid and mixed with unspiritual elements or one-sided or incomplete in its catholicity. For the transformation of the Ignorance into the integral Knowledge the growth in us of a spiritual intelligence ready to receive a higher light and canalise it for all the parts of our nature is an intermediate necessity of great importance."
The Life Divine, SABCL, Vol. 19, pp. 878-80

There's enough matter here to ask me at least a dozen questions! (*To a child*) So, the first of the twelve?

(*Silence*)

I have a question here, but it is a verbal question, which means that it is not very interesting. It is a phrase from the beginning of the passage: What is the meaning of "the mental consequences of the spiritual theorem of existence"?

It is probably from someone who doesn't know

what "theorem" means!

A theorem is the statement of a truth which has been arrived at through reasoning. The word is used quite concretely in mathematics and all the external sciences. From the philosophical point of view it is the same thing. In the present instance, the spiritual theorem of existence may be stated in this way: the Absolute in the relativities or Oneness in multiplicity. But to explain "the mental consequences", we must go into philosophy and I believe you are rather unprepared for that. And to really understand what it means, one feels that philosophy is always skirting the truth, like a tangent that draws closer and closer but never touches — that there is something that escapes. And this something is in truth everything.

To understand these things... there is only experience — to live this truth, not to feel it in the way the ordinary senses do but to realise within oneself the truth, the concrete existence of both states, simultaneously, existing together even while they are opposite conditions. All words can lead only to confusion; only experience gives the tangible reality of the thing: the simultaneous existence of the Absolute and the relativities, of Oneness and multiplicity, not as two states following each other and one resulting from the other, but as a state which can be perceived in two opposite ways depending on... the position one takes in relation to the Reality.

Words in themselves falsify the experience. To speak in words one must take not a step backwards but a step downwards, and the essential truth escapes. One must

On "The Evolution of the Spiritual Man"

use them simply as a more or less accessible path to reach the *thing* itself which cannot be formulated. And from this point of view no formulation is better than any other; the best of all is the one that helps each one to remember, that is, the way in which the intervention of the Grace has crystallised in the thought.

Probably no two ways are identical, everyone must find his own. But one must not be mistaken, it is not "finding" by reasoning, it is "finding" by aspiration; it is not by study and analysis, but by the intensity of the aspiration and the sincerity of the inner opening.

When one is truly and exclusively turned to the spiritual Truth, whatever name may be given to it, when all the rest becomes secondary, when that alone is imperative and inevitable, then, *one single moment* of intense, absolute, total concentration is enough to receive the answer.

The experience comes first, in this case, and it is only later, as a consequence and a memory that the formulation becomes clear. In this way one is sure not to make a mistake. The formulation may be more or less exact, that is of no importance, so long as one doesn't make a dogma out of it.

It is good for you, that is all that is needed. If you want to impose it on others, whatever it may be, even if it is perfect in itself, it becomes false.

That is why religions are always mistaken — always — because they want to standardise the expression of an experience and impose it on everyone as an irrefutable truth. The experience was true, complete in itself, convincing — for the one who had it. The formulation he made of it was excellent — for himself. But to want to impose it on others is a fundamental error which has altogether disastrous consequences, always, which always leads far, very far from the Truth.

That is why all the religions, however beautiful they may be, have always led man to the worst excesses. All the crimes, the horrors perpetrated in the name of religion are among the darkest stains on human history, and simply because of this little initial error: wanting what is true for one individual to be true for the mass or collectivity.

(Silence)

The path must be shown and the doors opened but everyone must follow the path, pass through the doors and go towards his personal realisation.

The only help one can and should receive is that of the Grace which formulates itself in everyone according to his own need.

1 October 1958

Sweet Mother, what is an ideal of moral perfection?

There are thousands of moral perfections. Everyone has his own ideal of moral perfection.

What is usually called moral perfection is to have all the qualities that are considered moral: to have no defects, never to make a mistake, never to err, to be always what one conceives to be the best, to have all the virtues — that is, to realise the highest mental conception: to take all the qualities — there are many, aren't there? — all the virtues, all that man has conceived to be the most beautiful, most noble, most true, and to live that integrally, to let all one's actions be guided by that, all the movements, all the reactions, all the feelings, all... That is living a moral ideal of perfection. It is the summit of man's mental evolution.

Not many people do it... but still... there have been some and there still are. This is what men usually take for the spiritual life. When they meet a man of this type, they say, "Oh! He is a great spiritual being." He may be a great saint, he may be a great sage but he is not a spiritual being.

And yet it is already very good and very difficult to realise this. And there comes a time in the inner evolution when it is very necessary to try to realise it. It is obviously infinitely higher than to be still guided by all one's impulses and ignorant outer reactions. It is to be already in a way the master of one's nature. It is even a stage through which one has to pass, for it is the stage when one begins to be the master of one's ego, when one is ready to let it fall away — it is still there but sufficiently weakened to be nearing its end. This is the last stage before crossing over to the other side, and certainly, if anyone imagines that he can go over to the other side without passing through this stage, he would risk making a great mistake, and of taking for perfect freedom a perfect weakness with regard to his lower nature.

It is almost impossible to pass from the mental being — even the most perfect and most remarkable — to the true spiritual life without having realised this ideal of moral perfection for a certain period of time, however brief it may be. Many people try to take a short-cut and want to assert their inner freedom before having overcome all the weaknesses of the outer nature; they are in great danger of deluding themselves. The true spiritual life, complete freedom, is something much higher than the highest moral realisations, but one must take care that this so-called freedom is not an indulgence and a contempt for all rules.

One must go higher, always higher, higher; nothing less than what the highest of humanity has achieved.

One must be capable of being spontaneously all that humanity has conceived to be the highest, the most beautiful, the most perfect, the most disinterested, the most comprehensive, the best, before opening one's spiritual wings and looking at all that from above as something which still belongs to the individual self, in order to enter into true spirituality, that which has no limits, which lives in an integral way Infinity and Eternity.

8 October 1958

Sweet Mother, will there not be any intermediary states between man and superman?

There will probably be many.

Man and superman? You are not speaking of the new supramental race, are you? Are you really speaking of what we call the superman, that is, man born in the human way and trying to transform the physical being he has received by his ordinary human birth? Are there any stages? — There will certainly be countless *partial* realisations. According to each one's capacity, the degree of transformation will differ, and it is certain that there will be a considerable number of attempts, more or less fruitful or unfruitful, before we come to something like the superman, and even those will be more or less successful attempts.

All those who strive to overcome their ordinary nature, all those who try to realise materially the deeper experience which has brought them into contact with the divine Truth, all those who, instead of turning to the Beyond or the Highest, try to realise physically, externally, the change of consciousness they have realised within themselves — all are apprentice-supermen. And there, there are countless differences in the success of their efforts. Each time we try not to be an ordinary man, not to live the ordinary life, to express in our movements, our actions and reactions the divine Truth, when we are governed by that Truth instead of being governed by the general ignorance, we are apprentice-supermen, and according to the success of our efforts, well, we are more or less able apprentices, more or less advanced on the way.

All these are stages, so... In reality, in this race to the Transformation, the question is to know which of the two will arrive first: the one who wants to transform his body in the image of the divine Truth, or the old habit of the body to go on disintegrating until it is so deformed that it can no longer continue to live in its outer integrality. It is a race between transformation and decay. For there are only two stopping-places, two things which can indicate to what extent one has succeeded: either success, that is to say, becoming a superman — then of course one can say, "Now I have reached the goal"... or else death. Till then, normally, one is "on the way".

It is one of these two things — either attaining the goal or a sudden rupture of life — which temporarily puts an end to the advance. And on the road each one has gone more or less far, but until one reaches the end one cannot say what stage one is at. It is the final step that will count. So only the one who comes a few hundred or thousand years later and looks back, will be able to say, "There was this stage and that stage, this realisation and that realisation...." That is history, it will be a historical perception of the event. Till then all of us are in the movement and the work.

How far have we gone and how far shall we go? It is better not to think too much about that, for it cripples you and you can't run well. It is better to think only about running and nothing else. That is the only way to run well. You look at where you want to go and put all your effort in the movement to go forward. How far you have gone is not your concern. I say, "This is history", it will come later. The historians of our effort will tell us — because perhaps we shall still be there — will tell us what we did, how we did it. For the moment what is necessary is to do it; this is the only thing that matters.

22 October 1958

"But this is not the standpoint from which the true significance of the spiritual evolution in man or the value of spirituality can be judged or assessed; for its real work is not to solve human problems on the past or present mental basis, but to create a new foundation of our being and our life and knowledge. The ascetic or other-worldly tendency of the mystic is an extreme affirmation of his refusal to accept the limitations imposed by material Nature: for his very reason of being is to go beyond her; if he cannot transform her, he must leave her. At the same time the spiritual man has not stood back altogether from the life of humanity; for the sense of unity with all beings, the stress of a universal love and compassion, the will to spend the energies for the good of all creatures, are central to the dynamic outflowering of the spirit: he has turned therefore to help, he has guided as did the ancient Rishis or the prophets, or stooped to create and, where he has done so with something of the direct power of the Spirit, the results have been prodigious. But the solution of the problem which spirituality offers is not a solution by external means, though these also have to be used, but by an inner change, a transformation of the consciousness and nature.

"If no decisive but only a contributory result, an accretion of some new finer elements to the sum of

the consciousness, has been the general consequence and there has been no life-transformation, it is because man in the mass has always deflected the spiritual impulsion, recanted from the spiritual ideal or held it only as a form and rejected the inward change. Spirituality cannot be called upon to deal with life by a non-spiritual method or attempt to cure its ills by the panaceas, the political, social or other mechanical remedies which the mind is constantly attempting and which have always failed and will continue to fail to solve anything. The most drastic changes made by these means change nothing; for the old ills exist in a new form: the aspect of the outward environment is altered, but man remains what he was; he is still an ignorant mental being misusing or not effectively using his knowledge, moved by ego and governed by vital desires and passions and the needs of the body, unspiritual and superficial in his outlook, ignorant of his own self and the forces that drive and use him.... Only a spiritual change, an evolution of his being from the superficial mental towards the deeper spiritual consciousness, can make a real and effective difference. To discover the spiritual being in himself is the main business of the spiritual man and to help others towards the same evolution is his real service to the race; till that is done, an outward help can succour and alleviate, but nothing or very little more is possible."

The Life Divine, SABCL, Vol. 19, pp. 883-85

Sweet Mother, how can someone who hasn't much spiritual capacity best help in this work?

I don't know whether one can say that anyone has much or little spiritual capacity. It is not like that.

To live the spiritual life, a reversal of consciousness is needed. This cannot be compared in any way with the different faculties or possibilities one has in the mental field. It may be said of someone that he hasn't much mental, vital or physical capacity, that his possibilities are very limited; in that case it may be asked how these capacities may be developed, that is, how new ones may be acquired, which is something rather difficult. But to live the spiritual life is to open to another world within oneself. It is to reverse one's consciousness, as it were. The ordinary human consciousness, even in the most developed, even in men of great talent and great realisation, is a movement turned outwards — all the energies are directed outwards, the whole consciousness is spread outwards; and if anything is turned inwards, it is very little, very rare, very fragmentary, it happens only under the pressure of very special circumstances, violent shocks, the shocks life gives precisely with the intention of slightly reversing this movement of exteriorisation of the consciousness.

But all who have lived a spiritual life have had the same experience: all of a sudden something in their being has been reversed, so to speak, has been turned suddenly and sometimes completely inwards, and also at the same time upwards, from within upwards — but it is not an external "above", it is within, deep, something other than the heights as they are physically conceived. Something has literally been turned over. There has been a decisive experience and the standpoint in life, the way of looking at life, the attitude one takes in relation to it, has suddenly changed, and in some cases quite definitively, irrevocably.

And as soon as one is turned towards the spiritual life and reality, one touches the Infinite, the Eternal, and there can no longer be any question of a greater or smaller number of capacities or possibilities. It is the *mental* conception of spiritual life which may say that one has more or less capacity to live spiritually, but this is not at all an adequate statement. What may be said is that one is more or less ready for the decisive and total reversal. In reality, it is the mental capacity to withdraw from ordinary activities and to set out in search of the spiritual life which can be measured.

But so long as one is in the mental field, in this state, as it were, on this plane of consciousness, one can't do much for others, either for life in general or for particular individuals, because one doesn't have the certitude oneself, one doesn't have the definitive experience, the consciousness has not been established in the spiritual world; and all that can be said is that they are mental activities which have their good and bad sides, but not much power and, in any case, not this power of spiritual contagion which is the only truly effective power.

The only thing that is truly effective is the possibility of transferring to others the state of consciousness in which one lives oneself. But this power cannot be invented. One cannot imitate it, cannot seem to have it; it only comes spontaneously when one is established in that state oneself, when one lives within it and not when one is trying to live within it — when one is there. And that is why all those who truly have a spiritual life cannot be deceived.

An imitation of spiritual life may delude people who still live in the mind, but those who have realised this reversal of consciousness in themselves, whose relation with the outer being is completely different, cannot be deceived and cannot make a mistake.

It is these people the mental being does not understand. So long as one is in the mental consciousness, even the highest, and sees the spiritual life from outside, one judges with one's mental faculties, with the habit of seeking, erring, correcting, progressing, and seeking once again; and one thinks that those who are in the spiritual life suffer from the same incapacity, but that is a very gross mistake!

When the reversal of the being has taken place, all that is finished. One no longer seeks, one sees. One no longer deduces, one knows. One no longer gropes, one walks straight to the goal. And when one has gone farther — only a little farther — one knows, feels, lives the supreme truth that the Supreme Truth alone acts, the Supreme Lord *alone* wills, knows and does through human beings. How could there be any possibility of error there? What He does, He does because He wills to do it.

For our mistaken vision these are perhaps incomprehensible actions, but they have a meaning and an aim and lead where they ought to lead.

(*Silence*)

If one sincerely wants to help others and the world, the best thing one can do is to be oneself what one wants others to be — not only as an example, but because one becomes a centre of radiating power which, by the very fact that it exists, compels the rest of the world to transform itself.

29 October 1958

"It is true that the spiritual tendency has been to look more beyond life than towards life. It is true also that the spiritual change has been individual and not collective; its result has been successful in the man, but unsuccessful or only indirectly operative in the human mass. The spiritual evolution of Nature is still in process and incomplete, — one might almost say, still only beginning, — and its main preoccupation has been to affirm and develop a basis of spiritual consciousness and knowledge and to create more and more a foundation or formation for the vision of that which is eternal in the truth of the spirit. It is only when Nature has fully confirmed this intensive evolution and formation through the individual that anything radical of an expanding or dynamically diffusive character can be expected or any attempt at collective spiritual life, — such attempts have been made, but mostly as a field of protection for the growth of the individual's spirituality, — acquire a successful permanence. For till then the individual must be preoccupied with his own problem of entirely changing his mind and life into conformity with the truth of the spirit which he is achieving or has achieved in his inner being and knowledge. Any premature attempt at a large-scale collective spiritual life is exposed to vitiation by some incompleteness of the spiritual knowledge on

its dynamic side, by the imperfections of the individual seekers and by the invasion of the ordinary mind and vital and physical consciousness taking hold of the truth and mechanising, obscuring or corrupting it. The mental intelligence and its main power of reason cannot change the principle and persistent character of human life, it can only effect various mechanisations, manipulations, developments and formulations. But neither is mind as a whole, even spiritualised, able to change it; spirituality liberates and illumines the inner being, it helps mind to communicate with what is higher than itself, to escape even from itself, it can purify and uplift by the inner influence the outward nature of individual human beings: but so long as it has to work in the human mass through mind as the instrument, it can exercise an influence on the earth-life but not bring about a transformation of that life. For this reason there has been a prevalent tendency in the spiritual mind to be satisfied with such an influence and in the main to seek fulfilment in other-life elsewhere or to abandon altogether any outward-going endeavour and concentrate solely on an individual spiritual salvation or perfection. A higher instrumental dynamis than mind is needed to transform totally a nature created by the Ignorance."

The Life Divine, SABCL, Vol. 19, pp. 885-86

Sweet Mother, what is the meaning of "spirituality... helps mind... to escape from itself"?

On "The Evolution of the Spiritual Man"

As long as the mind is convinced that it is the summit of human consciousness, that there is nothing beyond and above it, it takes its own functioning to be a perfect one and is fully satisfied with the progress it can make within the limits of this functioning, and with an increase of clarity, precision, complexity, suppleness, plasticity in its movements.

It always has a spontaneous tendency to feel very satisfied with itself and with what it can do, and if there were no greater force than its own, a higher power which irrefutably shows it its own limitations, its poverty, it would never make any effort to find its way out of all that by the right door: liberation into a higher and truer mode of being.

When the spiritual force is able to act, when it begins to have an influence, it jolts the mind's self-satisfaction and, by continuous pressure, begins to make it feel that beyond it there is something higher and truer; then a little of its characteristic vanity gives way under this influence and as soon as it realises that it is limited, ignorant, incapable of reaching the true truth, liberation begins with the possibility of opening to something beyond. But it must feel the power, the beauty, the force of this beyond to be able to surrender. It must be able to perceive its incapacity and its limitations in the presence of something higher than itself, otherwise how could it ever feel its own weakness!

Sometimes one single contact is enough, something that makes a little rent in that self-satisfaction; then the yearning to go beyond, the need for a purer light awaken, and with this awakening comes the aspiration to win them, and with the aspiration liberation begins, and one day, breaking all limits, one blossoms in the infinite Light.

If there were not this constant Pressure, simultaneously from within and without, from above and from the profoundest depths, nothing would ever change.

Even with that, how much time is required for things to change! What obstinate resistance in this lower nature, what blind and stupid attachment to the animal ways of the being, what a refusal to liberate oneself!

(*Silence*)

In the whole manifestation there is an infinite Grace constantly at work to bring the world out of the misery, the obscurity and the stupidity in which it lies. From all time this Grace has been at work, unremitting in its effort, and how many thousands of years were necessary for this world to awaken to the need for something greater, more true, more beautiful.

Everyone can gauge, from the resistance he meets in his own being, the tremendous resistance which the world opposes to the work of the Grace.

And it is only when one understands that *all* external things, all mental constructions, all material efforts are vain, futile, if they are not entirely consecrated to this Light and Force from above, to this Truth which is trying to express itself, that one is ready to make decisive progress. So the only truly effective attitude is a

On "The Evolution of the Spiritual Man"

perfect, total, fervent giving of our being to That which is above us and which alone has the power to change everything.

When you open to the Spirit within you it brings you a first foretaste of that higher life which alone is worth living, then comes the will to rise to that, the hope of reaching it, the certitude that this is possible, and finally the strength to make the necessary effort and the resolution to go to the very end.

First one must wake up, then one can conquer.

5 November 1958

"Spiritual truth is a truth of the spirit, not a truth of the intellect, not a mathematical theorem or a logical formula. It is a truth of the Infinite, one in an infinite diversity, and it can assume an infinite variety of aspects and formations: in the spiritual evolution it is inevitable that there should be a many-sided passage and reaching to the one Truth, a many-sided seizing of it; this many-sidedness is the sign of the approach of the soul to a living reality, not to an abstraction or a constructed figure of things that can be petrified into a dead or stony formula. The hard logical and intellectual notion of truth as a single idea which all must accept, one idea or system of ideas defeating all other ideas or systems, or a single limited fact or single formula of facts which all must recognise, is an illegitimate transference from the limited truth of the physical field to the much more complex and plastic field of life and mind and spirit....

"In the evolution of the spiritual man there must necessarily be many stages and in each stage a great variety of individual formations of the being, the consciousness, the life, the temperament, the ideas, the character. The nature of instrumental mind and the necessity of dealing with the life must of itself create an infinite variety according to the stage of development and the individuality of the seeker. But, apart from that, even the domain of pure spiritual

On "The Evolution of the Spiritual Man"

self-realisation and self-expression need not be a single white monotone, here can be a great diversity in the fundamental unity; the supreme Self is one, but the souls of the Self are many and, as is the soul's formation of nature, so will be its spiritual self-expression. A diversity in oneness is the law of the manifestation; the supramental unification and integration must harmonise these diversities, but to abolish them is not the intention of the Spirit in Nature."

The Life Divine, SABCL, Vol. 19, pp. 886-88

From the point of view of individual development and for those who are still at the beginning of the path, to know how to remain silent before what one does not understand is one of the things which would help most in the progress — to know how to remain silent, not only externally, without uttering a word, but also to know how to be silent within, so that the mind does not assert its ignorance with its usual presumptuousness, does not try to understand with an instrument that is incapable of understanding, that it may know its own weakness and open simply, quietly, waiting until the time has come for it to receive the light, because only the Light, the true Light, can give it understanding. It is not all that it has learnt nor all that it has observed nor all its so-called experience of life, it is something else which is completely beyond it. And until this something else — which is the expression of the Grace — manifests within it, if, very quietly, very modestly the mind remains silent and does not try to understand and, above all, to judge, things would go much faster.

The noise made by all the words, all the ideas in your head is so deafening that it prevents you from hearing the truth when it wants to manifest.

To learn to be quiet and silent... When you have a problem to solve, instead of turning over in your head all the possibilities, all the consequences, all the possible things one should or should not do, if you remain quiet with an aspiration for goodwill, if possible a need for goodwill, the solution comes very quickly. And as you are silent you are able to hear it.

When you are caught in a difficulty, try this method: instead of becoming agitated, turning over all the ideas and actively seeking solutions, of worrying, fretting, running here and there inside your head — I don't mean externally, for externally you probably have enough common sense not to do that! but inside, in your head — *remain quiet*. And according to your nature, with ardour or peace, with intensity or widening or with all these together, implore the Light and wait for it to come.

In this way the path would be considerably shortened.

ON "THE TRIPLE TRANSFORMATION"

12 November 1958

"If it is the sole intention of Nature in the evolution of the spiritual man to awaken him to the supreme Reality and release him from herself, or from the Ignorance in which she as the Power of the Eternal has masked herself, by a departure into a higher status of being elsewhere, if this step in the evolution is a close and an exit, then in the essence her work has been already accomplished and there is nothing more to be done. The ways have been built, the capacity to follow them has been developed, the goal or last height of the creation is manifest; all that is left is for each soul to reach individually the right stage and turn of its development, enter into the spiritual ways and pass by its own chosen path out of this inferior existence. But we have supposed that there is a farther intention, — not only a revelation of the Spirit, but a radical and integral transformation of Nature. There is a will in her to effectuate a true manifestation of the embodied life of the Spirit, to complete what she has begun by a passage from the Ignorance to the Knowledge, to throw off her mask and to reveal herself as the luminous Consciousness-Force carrying in her the eternal Existence and its universal Delight of being. It then becomes obvious that there is something not yet accomplished, there becomes clear to view the much that has still to be done, bhūri aspaṣṭa kartvam; *there is a height still to*

> *be reached, a wideness still to be covered by the eye of vision, the wing of the will, the self-affirmation of the Spirit in the material universe. What the evolutionary Power has done is to make a few individuals aware of their souls, conscious of their selves, aware of the eternal being that they are, to put them into communion with the Divinity or the Reality which is concealed by her appearances: a certain change of nature prepares, accompanies or follows upon this illumination, but it is not the complete and radical change which establishes a secure and settled new principle, a new creation, a permanent new order of being in the field of terrestrial Nature. The spiritual man has evolved, but not the supramental being who shall thenceforward be the leader of that Nature."*
> The Life Divine, SABCL, Vol. 19, pp. 889-90

Sweet Mother, how can one find the right stage and turn of one's development?

How can you find it!... You must look for it. You must want it persistently. It must be the important thing for you.

(*Silence*)

What happens most often when one makes the inner effort that's needed to discover one's soul, to unite with it and allow it to govern one's life, is a kind of marvellous enchantment with this discovery, as a result of which the first instinct is to tell oneself, "Now I have what I need, I have found infinite delight!" and no longer to be concerned with anything else.

In fact this is what has happened to almost all those who have made this discovery, and some of them have even set up this experience as a principle of realisation and said, "When you have done that, everything is done, there is nothing more to do; you have reached the goal and the end of the road."

Indeed, a great courage is necessary to go farther; this soul one discovers must be an intrepid warrior soul which does not at all rest satisfied with its own inner joy while comforting itself for the unhappiness of others with the idea that sooner or later everybody will reach that state and that it is good for others to make the same effort that one has made or, at best, that from this state of inner wisdom one can, with "great benevolence" and "deep compassion" help others to reach it, and that when everybody has attained it, well, that will be the end of the world and that's so much the better for those who don't like suffering!

But... there is a "but". Are you sure that this was the aim and intention of the Supreme when he manifested?

(Silence)

The whole creation, the whole universal manifestation appears at best like a very bad joke if it only comes to this. Why begin at all if it is only to get out of it! What is the use of having struggled so much, suffered so much, of having created something which, at least in its external appearance, is so tragic and dramatic, if it is simply to teach you how to get out of it — it would have been better not to begin at all.

But if one goes to the very depth of things, if, stripped not only of all egoism but also of the ego, one gives oneself totally, without reserve, so completely and disinterestedly that one becomes capable of understanding the plan of the Lord, then one knows that it is not a bad joke, not a tortuous path by which you return, a little battered, to the starting-point; on the contrary, it is to teach the entire creation the delight of being, the beauty of being, the greatness of being, the majesty of a sublime life, and the perpetual growth, perpetually progressive, of that delight, that beauty, that greatness. Then everything has a meaning, then one no longer regrets having struggled and suffered, one has only the enthusiasm to realise the divine goal, and one plunges headlong into the realisation with the *certitude* of the goal and victory.

But to know that, one must stop being egoistic, being a separate person turned in on oneself and cut off from the supreme origin. That is what must be done: to cast off one's ego. Then one can know the true goal — and this is the only way!

To cast off one's ego, to let it fall off like a useless garment.

The result is worth the efforts that must be made. And then, one is not all alone on the way. One is helped, if one has trust.

On "The Triple Transformation"

If you have had even a second's contact with the Grace — that marvellous Grace which carries you along, speeds you on the path, even makes you forget that you have to hurry — if you have had only a second's contact with that, then you can strive not to forget. And with the candour of a child, the simplicity of a child for whom there are no complications, give yourself to that Grace and let it do everything.

What is necessary is not to listen to what resists, not to believe what contradicts — to have trust, a real trust, a confidence which makes you give yourself fully without calculating, without bargaining. Trust! The trust that says, "Do this, do this for me, I leave it to You."

That is the best way.

26 November 1958

> "As Mind is established here on a basis of Ignorance seeking for Knowledge and growing into Knowledge, so Supermind must be established here on a basis of Knowledge growing into its own greater Light. But this cannot be so long as the spiritual-mental being has not risen fully to Supermind and brought down its powers into terrestrial existence. For the gulf between Mind and Supermind has to be bridged, the closed passages opened and roads of ascent and descent created where there is now a void and a silence. This can be done only by the triple transformation to which we have already made a passing reference: there must first be the psychic change, the conversion of our whole present nature into a soul-instrumentation; on that or along with that there must be the spiritual change, the descent of a higher Light, Knowledge, Power, Force, Bliss, Purity into the whole being, even into the lowest recesses of the life and body, even into the darkness of our subconscience; last, there must supervene the supramental transmutation, — there must take place as the crowning movement the ascent into the Supermind and the transforming descent of the supramental Consciousness into our entire being and nature."
>
> *The Life Divine*, SABCL, Vol. 19, pp. 890-91

What is the role of the spirit?

One might say that it is both the conscious intermediary between the Supreme and the manifestation, and the meeting-place of the manifestation with the Supreme.

Spirit is capable of understanding and communicating with the highest Godhead and at the same time it is the purest, one might say the least distorted intermediary of the highest Godhead in the outermost manifestation. It is spirit which, with the help of the soul, turns the consciousness towards the Highest, the Divine, and it is in the spirit that the consciousness can begin to understand the Divine.

It might be said that what is called "spirit" is the atmosphere brought into the material world by the Grace so that it may awaken to the consciousness of its origin and aspire to return to it. It is indeed a kind of atmosphere which liberates, opens the doors, sets the consciousness free. This is what enables the realisation of the truth and gives aspiration its full power of accomplishment.

From a higher standpoint, this could be put in another way: it is this action, this luminous and liberating influence that is known as "spirit". All that opens to us the road to the supreme realities, pulls us out from the mud of the Ignorance in which we are stuck, opens the doors to us, shows us the path, leads us to where we have to go — this is what man has called "spirit". It is the atmosphere created by the Divine Grace in the universe to save it from the darkness into which it has fallen.

The soul is a kind of individual concentration of this Grace, its individual representative in the human being. The soul is something particular to humanity, it exists only in man. It is like a particular expression of the spirit in the human being. The beings of the other worlds do not have a soul, but they can live in the spirit. One might say that the soul is a delegation of the spirit in mankind, a special help to lead it faster. It is the soul that makes individual progress possible. The spirit, in its original form, has a more general, more collective action.

For the moment the spirit plays the part of a helper and guide, but it is not the all-powerful master of the material manifestation; when the Supermind is organised into a new world, the spirit will become the master and govern Nature in a clear and visible way. What is called "new birth" is the birth into the spiritual life, the spiritual consciousness; it is to carry in oneself something of the spirit which, individually, through the soul, can begin to rule the life and be the master of existence. But in the supramental world, the spirit will be the master of this entire world and all its manifestations, all its expressions, consciously, spontaneously, naturally.

In the individual existence, that is what makes all the difference; so long as one just speaks of the spirit and it is something one has read about, whose existence one vaguely knows about, but not a very concrete reality for the consciousness, this means that one is not born into the spirit. And when one is born into the spirit, it becomes something much more concrete, much more living, much more real, much more tangible than the

On "The Triple Transformation"

whole material world. And this is what makes the essential difference between beings. When *that* becomes spontaneously real — the true, concrete existence, the atmosphere one can freely breathe — then one knows one has crossed over to the other side. But so long as it is something rather vague and hazy — you have heard about it, you know that it exists, but... it has no concrete reality — well, this means that the new birth has not yet taken place. As long as you tell yourself, "Yes, this I can see, this I can touch, the pain I suffer from, the hunger that torments me, the sleep that makes me feel heavy, this is real, this is concrete..." (*Mother laughs*), that means that you have not yet crossed over to the other side, you are not born into the spirit.

(*Silence*)

In fact, the vast majority of men are like prisoners with all the doors and windows closed, so they suffocate, which is quite natural. But they have with them the key that opens the doors and windows, and they do not use it.... Certainly there is a time when they don't know they have the key, but long after they have come to know it, long after they have been told about it, they hesitate to use it and doubt whether it has the power to open the doors and windows or even that it is a good thing to open them! And even when they feel that "after all, it might be good", there remains some fear: "What will happen when these doors and windows are opened?..." and they are afraid. They are afraid of being lost in that light and freedom. They want to remain what they call "themselves". They like their falsehood and their bondage. Something in them likes it and goes on clinging to it. They still have the impression that without their limits they would no longer exist.

That is why the journey is so long, that is why it is difficult. For if one truly consented to cease to exist, everything would become so easy, so swift, so luminous, so joyful — but perhaps not in the way men understand joy and ease. In truth, there are very few people who do not enjoy fighting. There are very few who could accept the absence of night, few can conceive of light except as the opposite of darkness: "Without shadows there would be no picture. Without struggle, there would be no victory. Without suffering there would be no joy." That is what they think, and so long as one thinks in this way, one is not yet born into the spirit.